The Revelation
GENERATION

The Revelation
GENERATION

PERRY STONE, JR.

Perry Stone
Voice of Evangelism
P.O. Box 3595
Cleveland, Tennessee 37320

Published in association with The Fedd Agency, Inc., a literary agency.

Unless otherwise noted, all scripture quotations are from the KJV, King James Version.

Scripture taken from the New King James Version®. Copyright © 1982 by Thomas Nelson. Used by permission. All rights reserved.

ISBN: 978-1-943217-51-9
Ebook: 978-1-943217-52-6

Printed in the United States of America
First Edition 15 14 13 10 09 / 10 9 8 7 6 5 4 3 2

TABLE OF CONTENTS

1. THE ERA OF THE CANDELABRA..9

2. SIX WOES OVER AMERICA:
WARNING PATTERN FROM ISAIAH..19

3. THE SIGN OF AMERICA'S FUTURE SHAKING........................51

4. AMERICA, WHAT HAPPENS WHEN GOD
STOPS WARNING US?..97

5. AMERICA: THE NEW ROMAN EMPIRE................................123

6. PATRIARCHS AND PROPHETS WHO FORESAW THE FUTURE........133

7. BIBLICAL NUMBERS AND THE HEBREW ALPHABET
REVEAL THE ELECTION CODES..161

8. THE DAYS FOR A YEAR THEORY AND
ISRAEL'S RESTORATION..193

9. PROPHECIES CONCEALED ON THE
JEWISH CALENDAR..211

10. PROPHECIES IN THE DEAD SEA SCROLLS........................221

11. THE BATTLE OVER THE MOUNTAIN OF GOD—
THE TEMPLE MOUNT CONTROVERSY................................239

12. WHAT DOES ALL OF THIS MEAN?......................................265

ENDNOTES..269

1.

THE ERA OF
THE CANDELABRA

"The visible return of the Messiah, Jesus Christ, to raise the righteous dead and transform those alive from mortals to immortality could not have occurred before the year 1948!"

This is a controversial statement to make, to say the least. After nearly forty years of comprehensive biblical research probing prophecies with a spiritual magnifying glass, to corroborate this statement, I released a teaching using this as the foundational thought during a major prophetic conference, only afterwards to hear a bit of opposing feedback, such as "I am not sure I agree" or "Christ could have returned for the church at any time before 1948," of which I gently reminded these sincere friends, "But we are still here, aren't we? Christ didn't come before 1948, did he?" The fact is, biblical predictions confirm that the Messiah would return only after specific events transpired, contrary to the majority of prophetic teachers' interpretations of events. There *are* specific signs foretold in the prophetic portion of Holy Scriptures that must be achieved as harbingers pointing to the Lord's return. They are related to both the rapture appearing (1 Thessalonians 4:16-17) and Christ's visible return to Jerusalem at the end of the tribulation, where he initiates his one-thousand-year earthly reign as King of Kings (Revelation 19:11-16). I have heard throughout my prophetic ministry that there are "no signs given in the New Testament that must be fulfilled before the rapture occurs." Many teachers often note that the majority of signs in Matthew 24, Mark 13, and Luke 21 are linked to the time of the great tribulation and not the rapture. However, this interpretation is only a partially correct assumption.

Two momentous "signs" will be indisputable evidence of Christ's return for the church—both colliding at once during what scholars call "the Church Age," also called the "dispensation of the grace of God" (Ephesians 3:2). First, the gospel must be "preached in all the world as a witness to all nations, then the end will come," followed by the great tribulation (Matthew 24:14-15). The gospel (good news of salvation) will be preached and taught by Christ's followers and his ministers, providing a salvation opportunity for the unsaved (Matthew 28:19-20). Thus, the return of Christ to gather together his body—the church (Ephesians 1:9-10)—will occur after all nations have access to the gospel. The second church-related prediction that precedes the return of Christ foretells that the Holy Spirit will be "poured out" on young and old (all flesh, KJV) in the "last days," inspiring the recipients to "prophesy." Dreams and visions will also become commonplace, and specifically identified cosmic evidence in the sun, moon, and stars will mark the timing of this outpouring accompanied by strange signs beneath the earth—blood, fire, and pillars of smoke (possibly volcanic eruptions). These combined indicators precede the "great and terrible day of the Lord," a prophetic phrase used to identify the future great tribulation" (Joel 2:28-29). This outpouring of the Spirit is the final "spiritual rain" necessary to soften the soil of men's hearts to receive the seed of God's Word, maturing new believers in the truth, in preparation for earth's final soul-harvest. James wrote: "Therefore be patient, brethren, until the coming of the Lord. See how the farmer waits for the precious fruit of the earth, waiting patiently for it until it receives the early and latter rain. You also be patient. Establish your hearts, for the coming of the Lord is at hand" James 5:7-8 (NKJV).

As the gospel is globally disseminated and the Holy Spirit pours his "rivers of living water" into human vessels (John 7:38-39), these two "pre-rapture signs" both will materialize at once during the climax of the Church Age and are made possible through believers preaching, teaching, and globally declaring the message of the gospel. Historically, in 1948, one month after Israel was reborn as a nation, Pentecostal historians marked the beginning of a great "Restoration Revival," whose ministers began preaching the return of Christ and a future outpouring of the Spirit, based on the sign of Israel's restoration. Most ministers lived to see the seed of their prediction bring forth a mighty harvest nineteen years later, in 1967, when what was termed the "Charismatic Renewal" erupted across North America, eventually spreading around the world. The month of June in 1967 was amazing—the same year that the Israelis regained all of Jerusalem, uniting the city under Israeli government supervision, recapturing the south (Gaza), the West Bank (Judea and Samaria), and the Golan Heights (the ancient Basham), restoring to the possession lands promised to Abraham's seed that were in the possession of often-antagonistic Gentile control or influence.

With all evidence now in, it was the Gregorian calendar year 1948 that was a divinely appointed *set time* we can mark as the starting point for the prophetic countdown leading toward Christ's return. Among informed prophetic students, 1948 is the starting point for what has been termed as "the beginning of the end."

THE EXODUS AND THE INGATHERING

In 1945, after the allies liberated thousands of Holocaust survivors, the Jewish refugees were fearful of returning to their Eastern European homes because of the destruction of their property and for fear of anti-Semitism still persisting in parts of Europe This was indicated in Poland where in 1946, during an anti-Jewish riot, Polish rioters in Kielce killed forty-two Holocaust survivors attempting to return to Poland. In 1944 the Jewish Brigade Group was formed, which assisted Holocaust survivors living in exile to return to Palestine. One ship called *Exodus 1947*, carrying 4,500 Holocaust survivors, was turned away at the Port in Haifa and sent back to Germany. The British, who held the mandate over Palestine, actually fought the return of the Jews to Palestine due to Arab objections, placing 50,000 Jewish refugees in a camp on the island of Cypress. However, from 1948 to 1952 an estimated 170,000 displaced Jews found a homeland in Israel. This was the beginning of the second Exodus, predicted by Jeremiah 16:14-15:

> "'Therefore behold, the days are coming,' says the LORD, 'that it shall no more be said, "The LORD lives who brought

up the children of Israel from the land of Egypt," but, "The LORD lives who brought up the children of Israel from the land of the north and from all the lands where He had driven them." For I will bring them back into their land which I gave to their fathers.'"

Thus, beginning in 1948 the ancient land called Israel received back thousands of the descendants of the sons of Abraham and Isaac, much to the dismay and anger of Palestinian Arabs and Arab nations. From that moment, many Arabs considered the Jews as illegal invaders and "Israel" an imaginative creation of the "Christian West" to advance their prophetic belief that the restoration of Israel would help to bring the Christian Messiah, Jesus, back to earth.

These antagonists of Israel were *wrong* on their first presumption and *partially correct* on their second opinion. Since the days of Abraham, who once walked the length and breadth of Canaan, his son, Isaac, was not only promised the land from the River of Egypt to the Euphrates (Genesis 15:18), but at one time they actually also possessed much of this promised land, even back in the days of David and Solomon, who expanded the Israelite kingdom. A thousand years later, in Christ's time, political puppets called Roman "governors" (Luke 2:2; Matthew 27:2) and the Roman legions, whose visible presence created silent intimidation, occupied the land, until finally the Roman Tenth Legion surrounded Jerusalem, destroying the Temple and city in 70 A.D. Herein is the miracle. After eighteen centuries, the Jews returned to their original home, not as occupiers but as settlers, as promised by the Hebrew prophets centuries before.

The speculation that Christians assisted politically and other ways in helping provide the means for the Jews to organize a homeland in their original land is undeniable. As you will read in this book, Jewish Zionism was becoming globally visible under Theodor Herzl in 1887, receiving some of its strongest backing not just from devout Jews, but also from individuals labeled "Zionist" Christians—citizens of Britain and America who believed the return of Jews to Palestine (a name I use in the book to describe the land prior to 1948) would be a major prophetic fulfillment, pointing to the soon return of Christ. Numerous Christian leaders were active publicly and privately, activating a strategy in 1947-1948 to restore a national homeland to the Jewish people. Among those advocating for the homeland was British-Christian General Edmund Allenby, who in December 1917 liberated Jerusalem, basing his strategy on Isaiah 31:4-5. British Lord Balfour guaranteed British support for a Jewish homeland in Palestine by penning the Balfour Declaration. Even American President Harry Truman, who behind a backdrop of a private, internal government controversy between he and General Marshall, went against the leaders in his administration, throwing his approval for the Jewish State. (This was after he was told by Jewish Zionist leaders that if he approved the decision, he would go down in history as being a "Cyrus"—the Persian king who permitted the Jews by a decree to return to Israel after seventy years in Babylonian captivity.)

As previously stated, it was no coincidence that in May 1948 David Ben-Gurion, Israel's first prime minister, himself a "Zionist," declared that Israel was now an independent state. This fulfilled a prediction that Zionist leader Herzl had written in his diary in 1898: "In fifty years, a Jewish state would be created." This national restoration also initiated an awesome revival, noted by Voice of Healing founder Gordon Lindsay, as the "Restoration Revival;" it hit America like a whirlwind. Beginning in 1948 noted ministers purchased huge, 10,000-seat tents, preaching messages on salvation, restoration, and healing. When news hit the newsstand of David Ben-Gurion's announcement that Israel was the name of the new Jewish state, there was an immediate resurgence and renewed interest in Bible prophecy, inspiring well-known ministers to paint large prophetic charts, hosting lectures and prophecy conferences, and often packing churches and auditoriums with curious seekers. The message was, "We are now in the last days, and prophecy is now being fulfilled." Since 1948, messages on Christ's return and the fulfillment of Bible prophecy have inspired millions of believers and challenged the unbelief of doubters.

The reason that 1948 is the most significant *prophetic year* since the year Christ was crucified is that no prophecy connected to the return of Christ, the rise of the Antichrist, and the tribulation could have been fulfilled until Israel was first a Jewish nation; Jerusalem, the Jewish capital and a city of global controversy, was in Jewish hands, and Jews were returning from Gentile nations to Israel. Biblical prophets taught that when Israel returns, the promised land will surrender its barren image, becoming a paradise of agricultural produce (Isaiah 35:1-7), drawing visitors like a magnet from around the world for spiritual pilgrimages to Jerusalem. None of these prophetic scenarios could have occurred until first, Israel was again an official Jewish-controlled nation with a legitimate government, an active economy, and a great army. Once Israel is rooted in the soil and resurrects from the womb of history, there will be a spiritual-moral decline experienced in the leading Gentile powers, such as America, as God's final attention focuses on a series of global judgments on Gentiles and removing the blindness on Israel to bring her people into a redemptive covenant with the Messiah (see Romans 11).

THE SIGN OF THE MENORAH

Zechariah was a prophet who envisioned numerous future events—in our time and beyond, centered in Israel and Jerusalem. These include Christ's visible return to the Mount of Olives and his position as King (Zechariah 12-14). In one vision Zechariah saw a seven-branched golden menorah with one olive branch on the left side and one branch on the right (Zechariah 4:2-6). This imagery is unique in relation to the symbolism of modern Israel. Most Westerners think that Israel's national symbol is the Megan David, better known as "the star of David," the six-pointed blue star embroidered on the white background of the Israeli flag. The Star of David symbol, a Jewish emblem since Medieval times, has been abused by Jewish haters, such as Hitler, to mark Jews from non-Jews during the Nazi Reign of Terror, but it is also an ancient emblem claimed by Jewish mystics as a protective seal that once marked the shields of David and Solomon, known as the Seal of Solomon. The Star of David is the emblem of the Israeli flag but *not* the national emblem of Israel.

Rabbinical interpretation of Zechariah 4:2-6 teaches that based upon the prophet's vision, Israel will know it has entered the time of the end when its people behold the menorah surrounded by olive branches. On this note, the official seal of the modern state of Israel after its restoration in 1948 is a menorah with an olive branch on each side! This emblem is on Israeli government stationery, as the menorah is the true emblem of Israel and uniquely also the emblem of the Gentile Church Age in Revelation 1-3, where Christ walks among the seven golden candlesticks.

In this book, we will explore numerous biblical and rabbinical prophecies, including ancient scrolls, journeying into the past to reveal how for 6,000 years, God has unlocked the future to patriarchs and prophets. We are now in the "set time" of Psalm 102:13, in which God is favoring Zion. I suggest that since 1948, the world has entered the *era of the Candelabra*, and this prophetic light now emanates across the world.

2.

SIX WOES OVER AMERICA: WARNING PATTERN FROM ISAIAH

Sin is a three-lettered word whose influence leads to eternal destruction, but the word *woe* is a three-lettered word that often precedes God's judgment. The word *woe* is used in Scripture in 106 places in ninety-eight verses. In the Old Testament several Hebrew words are translated into English as *woe*, whose meanings include a "crying out" such as saying "Oh" or "Alas." In these instances it's used as a form of lamentation. In the New Testament usage the "woe" often introduces or accompanies an expression of grief toward sin or injustice. Christ pronounced a "woe" against the hypocritical religious leaders, scribes, and lawyers of his time (see Matthew 24:13-29) and when placing curses upon the Galilean cities for their unbelief (Luke 10:13). A "woe" is never a positive word, but it is spoken to seize attention, hopefully turning individuals toward repentance.

Israel's lack of faith and inherent sin nature provoked God into warning the nation of the dangerous termination of their blessings if they persisted in walking in spiritual apostasy. These warnings were first penned on animal parchments by Moses in the wilderness. Written in Leviticus 26 and Deuteronomy 28 are a long series of what are termed "the blessings and the curses of the Law." God promised economic, agricultural, family, and spiritual blessing upon Israel if they would follow his Word and obey his commandments. Opposite results would occur if God's chosen people walked in sin and idolatry or willfully broke God's commandments without repenting of their sins. These curses included terror in the cities, the inability to defeat enemies in war, the invasion of enemies living inside their borders, droughts, famines, and food shortages (see Leviticus 26). The function of these "curses" was to permit negative circumstances that would discomfort God's rebellious people, thus turning them away from their disobedience to repentance and humility.

One of the strongest warnings Moses gave marked a future time when Israel would walk contrary to the covenant, breaking the commandments, and God would remove them from their land. These exiles did occur when the Assyrians seized the ten northern tribes, scattering them among the Gentile nations (note 1 Kings 11:30-35) and when the Babylonians destroyed the city, directing a Jewish captivity for seventy years (Jeremiah 50-51). A third exile was initiated after the Romans Tenth Legion destroyed Jerusalem and the Temple in 70 A.D., leaving Jerusalem a smothering, ruinous heap of burnt wood and toppled stones and forcing homeless Jews onto ships, chained as slaves, headed to Rome. Moses predicted these events centuries before they occurred:

"Your sons and your daughters shall

be given to another people, and your eyes shall look and fail with longing for them all day long; and there shall be no strength in your hand. A nation whom you have not known shall eat the fruit of your land and the produce of your labor, and you shall be only oppressed and crushed continually" (Deuteronomy 28:32-34 (NKJV)).

One of the unusual curses was when God said, "The alien that is among you shall rise higher and higher above you, and you shall come down lower and lower. He shall lend to you and not you to him. He shall be the head and you shall be the tail" (Deuteronomy 28:43). Any discerning American can see that this prediction seems applicable to our own nation as foreigners are taking many available jobs and are financed to start new businesses, while the government tax base provided by third- and fourth-generation working Americans is providing doles to massive numbers of people entering the nation.

God told Moses the time would come when Israel "would be in need of everything" (Deuteronomy 28:48), meaning they would have so many "needs" that could not be met. Our own parallel, in America, is that today we face the highest number of Americans in history who depend upon or require federal and state government aid for food stamps, welfare, and other necessities. And as more join the rolls, demanding more resources from state and federal agencies, the needs are clashing with the numbers, and the coffers are being tapped to the maximum, requiring higher tax revenues from the working public.

During this same discourse, Moses revealed an interesting prophetic statement that is also a part of a warning statement made by a parable of Christ in Matthew 21. Moses spoke of a time when Israel would provoke God with their idolatry, offering sacrifices to strange gods and eventually forgetting God (see Deuteronomy 32:15-18). When Israel turned from God, the Lord would raise up a new "nation" to follow him. Moses reprimanded them with this revelation: "I will move them to jealousy with those which are not a people; I will provoke them to anger with a foolish nation" (Deuteronomy 32:21).

Various words in this verse are repeated in the New Testament. Paul quoted this verse to Gentile believers in Rome, proving God had predicted that Gentiles would be accepted into the New Covenant, and this approval would provoke many devout Jews to jealousy. We read, "But I say did Israel not know? First Moses says; I will provoke you to jealousy by those who are not a nation, I will move you to anger by a foolish nation" (Romans 10:19). The "nation" alluded to here is the church, which consists of both believing Jews and Gentiles. Paul later states that the Gentiles are accepted in the covenant "to provoke them (the natural Jew) to jealousy" (Romans 11:11). The Christian church as the *nation* of which Moses spoke is confirmed with Peter's statement: the church is a "chosen generation, a royal priesthood, a holy nation, a peculiar people" (2 Peter 2:9). Peter is referring back to Moses' statement, which reads, "which in time past were not a people, but are now the people of God" (1 Peter 2:10).

This theme of a new nation coming to faith to replace the unbelieving religious sects in Israel for a season and to proclaim the gospel to the nations was not just a revelation to Paul and Peter, but was also earlier predicted by Christ himself.

Christ spoke a parable of a vineyard, over which the owner entrusted his servants to care for and steward. In the parable the overseers begin killing the servants assigned to care for the vineyard, eventually slaying the son of the owner. It's a clear picture of the prophets in ancient Israel being slain and a prediction of Christ's own death by the permission of the religious hierarchy. The Lord posed this question: "What should the owner of the vineyard do to the wicked men who slew his son?" The answer from the Pharisees was that the owner should give the vineyard to another group of servants who would produce fruit in their season. Then, these shocking words came from Christ to the Pharisees: "Therefore I say to you, the kingdom of God will be taken from you and given to a nation bearing the fruits of it. And whoever falls on this stone will be broken; but on whomever it falls, it will grind him to powder" (Matthew 21:24).

The primary meaning of a new "nation" bringing forth fruits refers to the birth and expansion of the New Testament church, which is a living, spiritual organism on earth, yet unseen by the Old Testament prophets, with the exception of Moses. The church began with 120, and today the Christian faith has an estimated 2.2 billion followers. The church is a *spiritual nation* dwelling within the world's *political nations*. We have our own set of rules (the Bible), our own ambassadors of the gospel (ministers, Ephesians 6:20), and our own language (new tongues, Mark 16:17 and Acts 2:4). Christ alone is the King over this kingdom (Revelation 19:16).

While the church is the fulfillment of Moses' prediction, history also indicates that God has raised up, in seasons, God-fearing and biblically founded nations to facilitate kingdom assignments. In the seventeenth century it was the British, a nation of people who in the earlier days emphasized that their kings and queens were in the lineage of Judah, through Tamar. The name "British," when transliterated from Hebrew, come from two words: *brith*, which means "covenant," and *ish*, the Hebrew word for "man." Thus, it was taught in earlier times in Britain that the original Anglo people in Britain were men of the covenant, tracing their royal lineage as far back as Judah and Tamar's son, Zarah (Genesis 38:29-30). It was King James I of England, who ruled from 1603 to 1635, who assigned forty-seven scholars to translate the Bible into the English language and completed the project in 1611. England and Scotland were active in sending missionaries, including the Scottish "medical missionary" David Livingstone, who moved to Africa in 1841 and is credited for both opening up much of Africa and celebrating in England when he returned for a season. Many English, American, and Scottish ministers who understood Bible prophecy also knew that one day the Jews would return to a homeland in Palestine. They often publicly expressed this premise.

In the last days of human empires, the leading Gentile nation that would contribute considerably to the Israel-homeland strategy and support Israel from its beginning to the present would be a *young lion* that evolved out of the *old* British lion, the United States of America. To me, a most unusual aspect of America is its amazing parallels between ancient Israel and the United States, especially in our early history. America is the only nation in world history that can boast of the same prophetic and spiritual patterns as Israel. For example:

• Both nations were born out of a divine plan of

God
- Both nations crossed a sea to get to their promised land
- Both nations had the land separated into thirteen divisions (Israel, tribes; America, colonies)
- Both nations possessed a land controlled by tribes (Israel, pagan tribes; America, Indians)
- Both nations removed tribes to possess the land (Israel, seven tribes; America, Indian tribes)
- Both nations had a city that belonged to no tribe (Israel, Jerusalem; America, Washington D.C.)
- Both nations had a division between the north and the south
- Both nations dealt with the area of Babylon (Israel, Babylon; America, Iraq)
- Both nations based their laws on Scripture, especially the Torah
- Both have experienced the same blessings and the same judgments

PROPHETS PARALLELS WITH AMERICA

Having researched and studied the Bible for over 150,000 hours, I have become a passionate student of biblical cycles, types, shadows, and repetitive prophetic parallels. Repetitive parallels were understood by Israel's wise King Solomon, who noted that "the thing which has been (in the past) is that which shall be" (Ecclesiastes 1:9-10). In my research, I have discovered that the same blessings that applied to Israel when they obeyed God are the same parallel blessings released to America when we honor God's Word and his covenant. However, if America rejects the ancestral covenant for the land, then the nation will experience the same disfavor and selective judgment that Israel incurred.

In the final years prior to Babylon's invasion of Judea and Jerusalem and the year before Jerusalem's destruction by Roman legions in 70 A.D., events have a striking resemblance with the spiritual, moral, and economic conditions evident in the United States. Years before the swarming army of Babylonia thundered across the dusty Judean mountains toward Jerusalem, the prophet Jeremiah warned the Judean king, the temple priests, and other timid prophets that God would remove his protection over Jerusalem, and the Babylonians would chain the Judeans, marching them back to Babylon for seventy years (Jeremiah 25:11). The problem with Jeremiah's warning was that economic prosperity was at a peak, and the dwellers in Jerusalem were living free from oppression. The priesthood was so comfortable and complacent that leading priests threatened to kill Jeremiah for his negative warnings of impending judgment. The contention was, *Jeremiah's warning of judgment did not match the present situation!*

This same spirit of mocking permeates America's contemporary culture, especially when those who verbally warn America for shedding innocent blood and mocking traditional covenants are lambasted as "stupid," or "fear mongers," and at times are physically threatened by radicals whose brains have simmered in the grease of biblical hatred. These radicals cook up phrases as "intolerant," hoping to verbally intimidate believers into swallowing their rubbished reasoning, with the intent of shutting the mouths of a righteous remnant. Jeremiah was harassed and *intimidated* by his peers, but in the end his predictions *dominated* as the priests were on the wrong side of prophecy, and Jeremiah lived out what he saw coming.

STRANGE SIGNS OF JERUSALEM'S DESTRUCTION

In 66 A.D., precisely four years prior to the Roman destruction of Jerusalem, there were numerous cosmic signs, many falling on Jewish festivals, that indicated that God's favor was being removed from the city. This included supernatural light at the ninth hour (three o'clock in the morning) shining in the Temple during the Feast of Unleavened Bread and shining around the brass altar for thirty minutes, making the night look as bright as day. A second prodigy was when the eastern gate of the inner court opened and closed by itself at the sixth hour of the night (midnight). This gate was heavy, made of brass, and one gate alone was sixty feet by twenty-three feet and normally took twenty men to open and close with great difficulty. A watchman was sent and assigned to shut it. Some within the Temple falsely believed God was closing the door on Israel's enemies, while others perceived God was departing from the Temple and leaving it unguarded. There were also false prophets predicting that God would not allow Jerusalem to fall, but God would intervene and destroy the Romans. This removal of a protective hedge was confirmed with another strange sign, when during the festival of Pentecost, as the priest was making his way into the inner court at night, they suddenly felt a quaking and heard a great noise followed by a voice saying, "Let us depart from hence." This was read by the wise men that the Temple would soon be destroyed.

One man, Jesus, son of Ananias, a simple plebeian and husbandman, four years before the war, during a time of great prosperity and peace, began crying out during the Festival of Tabernacles a proclamation against Jerusalem and the Holy House. It was against the brides and bridegrooms and "against this whole people." The elite in Jerusalem were offended at his cries and had the man beaten. Yet afterwards, he continued to lament the coming destruction of the city and the Temple. He uttered warnings for four years every day, saying, "Woe to Jerusalem." His cry was the "loudest at the festivals," and he continued for seven years and five months, "without growing hoarse or being tired." After one last cry, which ended with the words "Woe unto myself," he was struck by a stone from a Roman catapult and "gave up the Ghost."[1]

The Jewish historian Josephus, who personally saw events prior to and the moment of the destruction of the Temple, wrote that there were false prophets who were "infatuated, without either eyes to see or minds to consider, [who] did not regard the denunciations that God had made against them."[2] There were men among the Jews who considered these strange cosmic and Temple signs to be a witness of God's *favor* upon the Jews and his *disfavor* upon the Romans. Wise men among them, however, knew that God had departed the Temple, and the city would be destroyed. Two opinions clashed: one believed the signs were good news, and the other group discerned them as bad news for the city. The second group discerned properly.

Today, there are thousands of believers receiving warnings in visions and dreams for the United States who are being ignored not only by those in high political positions but also by ministers and "well-educated" church members. Those true visionaries walking in the fear of the Lord are often rejected by the mainline church in the same manner the prophets of the Bible were mocked.

Among the priests ministering during the second temple period there was a dangerous *false sense of security* salting the conscience of these religious leaders, blinding them like a lone candle's fading light in a darkening room to the obvious and impending danger. Thus, Israel's spiritual leaders incorrectly assumed that God's love for Jerusalem was unconditional to the point that he would never permit the city and the Holy House to be destroyed again, as occurred in the days of Jeremiah. However, Christ had forewarned his disciples that within *one generation* the Temple would again be destroyed, leaving Jerusalem a bleak, lonely, uninhabited skeleton of what it once was (see Matthew 24:1-3).

SIX WOES PARALLEL WITH MODERN AMERICA

America and Israel have parallel historical patterns, laws based upon the Torah, and principles of practical living founded upon Scripture. While certainly not every Israeli or American acknowledges the Bible, the earliest history of the Israel of antiquity runs amazingly on the same track as early American history.

Since America was founded on the Torah principles of judicial judgments, legislative law, and spiritual principles, then God has the "legal" right to weigh America as a nation according to the judgments revealed to Moses in the Torah! The eternal Word of God that released Israel's blessings or curses can also today be released from the printed page of the Holy Writ to an active circumstance, exalting (blessing) or debasing (cursing) America politically, economically, and spiritually. Israel was impacted for good when they walked in righteous paths, but it encountered negative and frightening internal and external conflicts when people slid downward on the road of disobedience.

Many years prior to the invasion of Nebuchadnezzar's

military brigades, Isaiah not only warned all of Judea of the coming danger, but it also announced six "woes," revealed by divine revelation, of the reasons God was going to permit destruction to strike the homeland. These were pre-judgment woes, and today the United States stands in the shadow of ancient Israel, ignoring the same warnings.

In Isaiah 5, the prophet gave a parable to Israel, comparing Israel to a vineyard. These six "woes" are recorded in this parable. It is interesting that Christ also presented his Jewish audience a vineyard parable in which he predicted that another nation would replace unbelieving Israel (Matthew 21). This same vineyard passage in Isaiah 5 was significant after the Civil War, as during Lincoln's second inaugural at his swearing-in, the Chief Justice marked Lincoln's Bible at Isaiah 5:27-28, which Lincoln kissed. It would be forty-one days later that Lincoln would be assassinated.

When carefully reviewing the six woes listed in Isaiah 5, these six prophetic warnings and parallels seem to manifest in America in the 1950s and carry over into our present time. It appears that about every ten years, another "woe" pattern emerges as the people in America continue to stray from the original covenant of their ancestors.

THE FIRST WOE OF MATERIALISM

"Woe to those who join house to house; they add field to field, till there is no place where they may dwell alone in the midst of the land! In my hearing the LORD of hosts said, 'Truly, many houses shall be desolate, great and beautiful ones, without inhabitant'"
- Isaiah 5:8-9

With the end of World War II and the conclusion of the

Great Depression, America was ready for an economic boom. The 1950s were noted as the decade of "post-war prosperity." Special G.I. bills made purchasing homes possible, along with educational and monetary benefits available for veterans. Factories began filling the landscape, hiring tens of thousands of new workers. America's fruit of her prosperity blessed the world with new products that were globally desired, increasing our exports. In the 1950s there was no trade competition from China or any Asian nation as America was a *producing*, and not just a *purchasing*, nation. The steel, auto, furniture, clothing, and food industries boomed, and investments were made in new homes and the development of suburbs. Historians use the word *boom* to describe the 1950s.

As prosperity expanded, it enabled Americans to own their own homes, automobiles, radios, televisions, and other material goods. Many factories constructed in the Southeast created an economic goldmine for smaller communities. The warning by Isaiah is that if the people become consumed in their materialism, in time, the houses would become empty and without inhabitants. Fifty years later, when the sub-prime mortgage crisis erupted, the dam broke, and America's housing industry sunk under the water of bank greed. In the 1933 Great Depression, about one thousand home loans were being foreclosed upon by banks daily. January 2007 to December 2011 saw more than 4 million complete foreclosures and more than 8.2 million starts.[3] Unrestrained love for things creates a spirit of materialism, and "things" can become a form of idolatry that stirs a person's desire for more and more "stuff."

THE SECOND WOE OF THE PARTY LIFE

"Woe to those who rise early in the morning, that they may follow intoxicating drink; who continue until night, till wine inflames them! The harp and the strings, the tambourine and flute, and wine are in their feasts; but they do not regard the work of the LORD, nor consider the operation of His hands"
- Isaiah 5:11-18

This second woe fits the scenarios of the 1960s perfectly. On January 29, 1919, with the ratification of the eighteenth amendment, America entered thirteen years (1920-1933) of prohibition, banning the sales and distribution of all alcoholic beverages. The amendment was repealed on December 5, 1933. Prohibition never quenched men's desire for alcohol. To fill in the gap, the Mafia and other criminal elements secretly produced what was called "the devil's brew," selling it on the black market. In the Southeast, especially the mountains of West Virginia, Tennessee, and Kentucky, "moonshining" became a popular activity as men forged copper "moonshine stills," generating their own hard liquor for purchase and transporting it across state lines. The Internal Revenue Service (IRS) sent agents to expose the stills, destroying them and arresting and fining moonshiners. Prohibition was later repealed as federal and state governments acknowledged they could raise huge tax revenues by legalizing alcohol and permitting companies to brew beers, make wines, and distill hard liquors, thus bringing large amounts of tax revenue into the government coffers.

In the 1960s drinking alcohol became common and acceptable among youth, initiating in America a culture of partying, with alcoholic beverages as an acceptable feature of social events. In the Isaiah woe, observe the numerous instruments and music that accompany drunkenness. This is evident in the 1960s as America's style of music changed from rhythm and blues to a new form called "rock and roll." The new catch phrase was "sex, drugs, and rock and roll." The mix of prosperity from the 1950s with the flippant entertainment lifestyle of the 1960s mirrors Isaiah's warning: when mixing drunkenness and music, people forget God. It was also in the early 1960s that prayer and Bible reading were removed from public schools, leaving future generations in spiritual ignorance.

In verse thirteen of the second woe there is this statement: "Honorable men are famished." Before the 1960s, men serving in any of the four branches of the United States military were publicly honored and highly respected for their service to the country. However, in the sixties, during the time of the Vietnam War, university campuses and large gatherings of young antiwar protestors dishonored all men in military service, burning the American flag and calling soldiers murderers and child-killers to the glee and enjoyment of the left-leaning media. Isaiah said the honorable men were "famished." The Hebrew word *famished* is *ra'ab*, meaning "to hunger." However, the word is also translated as "to suffer." No group of veterans has suffered more anguish, mockery, and disrespect than the Vietnam vets, who were dishonored by angry protestors in the very land they were sworn to protect. The 1960s reflect Isaiah's second woe.

THE THIRD WOE OF DEFIANT SKEPTICISM

"Woe to those who draw iniquity with cords of vanity, and sin as

if with a cart rope; That say, Let Him make speed and hasten His work, that we may see it; and let the counsel of the Holy one of Israel draw near and come, that we may know it"
- Isaiah 5:18-19

The third woe appears to have an application to the next decade, the 1970s, where a new defiance in God was introduced following the Vietnam War. The fires of this defiance were stroked by liberal professors in America's leading universities, especially in the Northeast. Soon a new concept, that "God is dead," emerged in public discussion at the same time that the belief of the biblical creation narrative was challenged. This all gave a new path for the theory of evolution to be paved in public school classrooms.

Sin became more open and more acceptable. Since some took the baited lie that "God was dead," their attitude toward sin (since this invisible deity had ceased to exist) was that iniquity is only the opinion of religious brainwashing. Morals are optional, and "sin" is an obsolete expression replaced by a new tolerance. It was a "do-your own-thing" decade. An entire generation of youth and adults began dragging around a *cart* of sin, defying God to restrain their sexual liberty. In 1973, the Supreme Court voted to legalize abortion, and abortion carts were placed in clinics to remove the pieces of infants from rooms. It was during this same time that a new sexual revolution was released, spreading sexually transmittable diseases. The 1970s was a decade of defiant skepticism toward God, the Bible, and the traditional Christian faith.

THE FOURTH WOE OF REVERSAL OF VALUES

*"Woe to those who call evil good, and good evil; who put darkness
for light, and light for darkness; who put bitter for sweet,
and sweet for bitter!"*
- Isaiah 5:20

The prosperity of the 1950s and the sexual revelation of
the 1970s, along with the removal of prayer and Bible
reading in public schools, created a spiritual void that
depleted spiritual values. The combination initiated a reversal of values that were contrary to the judicial, moral,
and biblical disciplines. This reversal of values weakened
the marriage covenant, as traditional thinking was taboo,
and new points of view toward divorce were admonished.
The battle of the 1980s included a challenge against any
longstanding biblical belief as it related to traditional up-
bringing, marriage, and family. Sex education was prolif-
erated in public schools, and in some "educational circles"
youth were encouraged to experiment with their sexuality
to "discover who they were." It was also the time when the
gay community boldly came out of the closet and, using
media propaganda including movies and sitcoms, began
pounding the message of same-sex relations as an alternative to traditional marriage.

Today any government employee who refuses to sign
the marriage certificate of a same-sex couple can be ar-
rested. If a person's speech is deemed negative toward
someone's sexual orientation, their opinions can be tagged
as "hate speech." Today a conservative Christian is classi-
fied as a possible domestic terror threat while the liberals
are coddled for their tolerance in allowing anyone from
anyplace to enter the nation, despite the fact that terror-

ists are entering the country. Evil is now permissible, and good is now rejected as "religious intolerance." Thus, the sweet is bitter, and the bitter is sweet, and the dark is called light, and the light is considered dark. These reversal of values is the fourth woe.

THE FIFTH WOE OF CONCEIT AND CONTEMPT FOR GOD

"Woe to those who are wise in their own eyes,
and prudent in their own sight!"
- Isaiah 5:21

Isaiah continues his woeful warnings in verse 21, where the prophet gives a clear observation that is today parallel to the United States. He foresaw an arrogance that would permeate men's ego. God warned, "Woe to them that are wise in their own eyes, and prudent in their own sight." Observant and discerning believers see this self-appointed pride often manifest itself among national leaders who refuse to follow the wise advice or warnings of others and instead believe their own reports from media puppets. These inner circle "yes men" continually swell the heads of their boss with bragging reports, accompanied by printed charts with red arrows from opinion polls pointing up, and prove they alone have solo wisdom in any national or global decision. For example, I recall hearing the former president of the United States declare that the greatest threat to mankind is "global warming," now called "climate change." Many scientists who disagree on climate change are ridiculed and mocked by those who believe the planet will soon fall apart and refuse to hear any facts disproving their climate change theories.

When America's forty-fourth president was elected, public statements were made that shocked many God-fearing Americans. While visiting Turkey, the president told a Muslim audience, "America is not a Christian nation." For the first three out of five years, he did not recognize the Christian-sponsored National Day of Prayer but willingly celebrated the yearly Islamic Ramadan White House dinner, instead honoring the Islamic tradition that Gabriel gave Mohammad in the Quran. The most negative mark against the forty-fourth president from a purely biblical perspective was his promotion of the legalizing of same-sex marriage. He thus legalized a biblical abomination.

Isaiah notes in verse twenty-three, men "justify the wicked for reward." There have been instances when outright criminals were hailed as heroes by protesting multitudes, while those defending the cities were labeled "pigs" and "evil." On one occasion, a thief broke into a home, and the owner did his civil duty to protect his house and family by shooting and injuring the intruder. What stunned the city was when the thief sued the owner for shooting him! This arrogant defiance and pride leads to the sixth woe.

THE SIXTH WOE OF PERVERTED JUSTICE— THE COURTS PERVERTED

"Woe to men mighty at drinking wine, woe to men valiant for mixing intoxicating drink, who justify the wicked for a bribe, and take away justice from the righteous man"
- Isaiah 5:22

The founding fathers of America were so concerned about the abuse of power within a democracy and the fact that a wrong "tyrant" leader in charge would pervert justice for their own personal pleasures that they divided the authority of the government into three separate branches: judicial, legislative, and executive. Isaiah warned of perverted justice, which became evident in the 1990s to the present.

While it is illegal for a politician to accept a bribe, there are loopholes around law. During an election year, businesses send checks to politicians to assist in their election campaigns. Once elected, the politician is then obligated to the giver of the gift and can be reminded that without the large campaign contributions, he would not be enjoying his high office. Election cash motivates special favors. Moses wrote about righteous judgment and the rules for righteous justice in Israel. He said, "You shall take no gift, for a gift blinds the wise and perverts the words of the righteous" (Exodus 23:8). The Hebrew word for "bribe," used in 1 Samuel 12:3 and Amos 5:12, is the same spelling as the word *kippur*, translated as "atonement." The three Hebrew letters are *kuf, pay*, and *resh*.

Why would the word *bribe* conceal the idea of "atonement" or the "expiation" of something? One observation is how some in the Italian Mafia, after dealing drugs, running prostitution, and setting up crime syndicates, will set aside a large amount of money at their death to ensure that the priest will pray them out of purgatory into heaven. A political bribe is used to cover for a possible negative situation in the future or when the gift giver needs special attention or intervention down the road; thus, a bribe is the umbilical cord from the giver to the receiver. It "covers" (atones) for the future. History has exposed the power of a bribe when a contributor to a politician was later given a huge government contract, which was proven to be a "payback" for a huge election year contribution from the donor. During the 2008 and 2012 elections, one political party provided free phones to voters, which certainly could motivate recipients to vote for such a "caring" and compassionate candidate.

My father is from the small town of War in McDowell County, West Virginia. Among the older mountain folks, McDowell country was noted, as far back as the 1940s, as being the most politically corrupt county in West Virginia. As a child, my father recalled how the sheriff would purchase small bottles of whiskey and wrap them with a five-dollar bill. He would send people door to door, handing out a free "gift," and the givers reminded the person to "vote a straight Democrat ticket on election day." This is a clear example of perverted justice and bribery, yet at that time, no one was complaining since most of the working men in McDowell were coal ministers, and the United Mine Workers always voted Democrat.

In verse twenty-four, the people have "cast away the law of the Lord of hosts and despised the word of the Holy One of Israel." The phrase "cast away" in Hebrew means "to reject," "to spurn," or "to disappear." Never in the history of America have so many shunned the commandments of God, treating the Bible equal to some obscure, ancient, outdated document, allegedly filled with errors. The rules of our culture have changed, and we are told we must adjust to the times, even if it requires challenging and changing our religious beliefs. The woes of Isaiah end with a warning that God himself will stretch forth his hand against the rebellious people.

When the warnings in all six woes begin occurring at the same time, God will then release an "ensign" to the nations (see Isaiah 5:26). There are numerous interpretations as to the ensign that God is speaking of. The Hebrew word for ensign is *nec*, which normally refers to a "flag or a banner" or a "military standard." However, the wording in Isaiah 5:27-29 is very similar in content and word imagery as Joel chapter 1, Joel being the prophet who predicted the restoration of Israel and the great end time's Holy Spirit outpouring. Isaiah said this future army would not be weary and alludes to the roaring of a lion. It is similar imagery painted by Joel who spoke of a great end-time army and an outpouring of the Holy Spirit (see Joel chapters 1 and 2).

One of the final signs indicating both the "last days" and the soon return of the Messiah is when the Holy Spirit is poured out globally—on sons and daughters and old and young (See Joel 2:28-29). This unleashing of God's Spirit, according to the New Testament, is accompanied by a visible "sign," called "speaking with other tongues" (Acts 2:1-4). Paul specifically called this manifestation a "sign" for the unbeliever (1 Corinthians 14:22). The point is, while the world will slip toward the abyss of billowing darkness, the true believer will burn brighter with the light of the glorious gospel, being confirmed with mighty signs and wonders!

A SILENT HEAVEN—HEADING TOWARD DISASTER

Some danger signs indicating God's displeasure with a nation's behavior are concealed in events recorded in Israel's early history in the time of Samuel. In the years prior to the selection of Saul, Israel's first king, the once-active voice of God, heard by the patriarchs and early prophets, that burned their ears with illumination, suddenly went deafening silent for a season. The same was true hundreds of years later when the last Hebrew prophet Malachi warned Israel for disrespecting God's divine order at the Temple. When Malachi laid down his quill pen after writing his last verse, God stopped talking to Israel for 400 years. According to rabbis, God's audible voice ceased from echoing his word across the celestial world to the terrestrial realm. Christian scholars acknowledge this 400-year silence and note that it was broken when a wild man from the Judean wilderness, John the Baptist, become a prophetic voice assigned to introduce the Messiah. The days of Samuel, however, paint a reflection of the spiritual and political malignancy, eating away internally America's foundation that made her the greatest Gentile influence in modern history. *Our danger, as in Samuel's time, is our national and spiritual leaders' inability to hear and discern the voice of God.*

America is filled with teaching voices, spiritual gurus now called "life coaches," encouraging the masses to have a better life now. They teach how to be successful in business, and Christian television is now a plethora of practical living advisors. However, where is the powerful, life-changing gospel with piercing conviction leading to radical conversions? There is a shortage of men and women with prophetic visions, with their ears vibrating and heart pounding after hearing God's voice from the jasper throne—listening, then delivering the convicting messages and warnings from God. I am not speaking of self-appointed and self-anointed prophets and prophetesses who yelp like carnival barkers, using their gift to manipulate God's sheep into playing the game of "sowing a bigger seed for a bigger harvest" and whose "prophetic words" always come back around to financial blessings based on the number of zeros printed on your money. I have known of men to write letters to their mailing lists or say that financial blessings will *only* follow those giving

41

to *their* ministry! These "green back" blessings oddly are always based on the *amount* released from a giver's wallet or a woman's checkbook. These techniques that at time borderline on manipulation can be "merchandising of the gospel," and Peter exposed these *prophets for profit* in his day and warned his readers to beware of them and not be taken in by their feigned words and promises (2 Peter 2:3). I am asking, *Where are the Leonard Ravenhills, Steve Hills, and David Wilkersons, who burned for God, willing to pen words on paper and declare prophetic warnings to an earless generation who has selective deafness when hearing any call to repentance?*

THE SIGN OF THE RIGHTEOUS DEPARTING

Here is an ignored sign that America is headed toward a dangerous time*: when the true prophets are taken from us and are not replaced by others carrying their mantle.* Moses transferred his mantle to Joshua, then Joshua appointed elders. By the third generation, there arose a generation who "knew not God," and the people turned toward idolatry (Joshua 2:8-11). Joshua carried Moses' anointing, but no one picked up Joshua's mantle. Thus, Joshua's leadership mantle dissolved at his death. There were ten righteous men, all who lived long lives, prior to Noah's flood (Genesis 5). Before the fountains of the deep erupted and heaven pounded the earth with forty days of rain making earth one large ocean, all of the righteous men died, except one . . . Noah. The book of Jasher (a book mentioned in Joshua 10:13 and 2 Samuel 1:18) was translated from a copy found in 1840 into English and gives the year each righteous man died:

- In the 84th year of Noah's life Enos died

- In the 179th year of Noah's life Canian died
- In the 195th year of Noah's life Lamech died
- In the 234th year of Noah's life Mahalallel died
- In the 336th year of Noah's life Jared died[4]

—Jasher Chapters 4 and 5

The last antediluvian who died just before the flood was the great, great grandfather of Noah, Methuselah, who lived 969 years (Genesis 5:27). This godly patriarch died seven days before the first raindrop fell. God allowed Noah to bury this dear relative, which is why God said, "Yet seven days I will cause it to rain" (Genesis 7:4). He allowed time for Noah to bury and grieve—one week— for his loyal relative. The reasons why God permitted the deaths of these righteous men prior to the earth's eradication of sin is: "And all who followed the Lord died in those days before they saw the evil which God did declare to do upon the earth" (Jasher 5:5).

An implication from this insight is that evil was so loathsome, and men were such reprobates spreading corruption across the earth, that God was removing the godly to prevent them from being grieved and lamenting over the judgment he was declaring. After all, many of those who would be destroyed were families who had emerged out of the lineage of these righteous men. Knowing that hundreds or thousands of your relatives would drown would be a heavy burden to bear. Thus, they departed this life before the deluge. Sacred Jewish history says that in the 480th year of Noah's life, all the righteous men except Methuselah died (Jasher 5:6). This departure of the righteous before the flood is mentioned again in Jasher 5:21: "And all the sons of men who knew the Lord died in that year before the Lord brought evil upon them; for the

Lord willed them to die so as not to behold the evil that God would bring upon their brothers and relatives as he declared so."

When godly, righteous men and spiritual leaders are taken from us and not replaced, evil men are often unrestrained from seizing the reins of control in nations that once knew God. Righteous people restrain the cancerous spread of evil. A similar parallel with the days of Noah is centuries later repeated in Egypt with the sons of Jacob.

The same book of Jasher records the exact year when each of Jacob's twelve sons died in Egypt (Jasher chapter 61 and 62). Jacob's last son living in Egypt who died ninety-three years after entering Egypt was Levi. After his departing, the Egyptians began afflicting the Hebrews, harassing them, and taking their vineyards, lands, and houses that Joseph had given them. About this time, a new Pharaoh arose who did not know the history of Israel and Joseph (see Exodus 1:8). This new king began forcing the Hebrews to work under his tyrannical dictatorship, making the people slaves to the government of Egypt.

America's new form of Christianity promotes "spiritual guides" who encourage silence over conflict and tolerance to snuff out any negative preaching as a sign of "real love" toward those we may disagree with. However, truth can only transform when it is known, and without powerful preaching the voice of reason and repentance becomes an echo, eventually fading into the sunset of memory. Isaiah observed why, at times, the pure-hearted and spiritually devoted, or righteous, were taken: "The righteous perishes, and no man lays it to heart: and merciful men are taken away, none considering that the righteous is taken away from the evil to come" (Isaiah 57:1).

Said another way, previous generations of Christians

who are now with the Lord in heaven would not believe how far America has fallen from its pinnacle of spirituality and morality. My own grandfather, who survived the Great Depression, and my father, who was a teenager during the Korean war, before their deaths were shocked at the total decline in America's values and lack of moral clarity. These "old-timers" would come out of their graves screaming at this apostate generation.

SILENCE OF THE PROPHETIC VOICES

A rather sad observation is the number of men globally recognized as carrying a mantle of prophetic influence who have all—within a ten-year timeframe—gone to heaven, some within months of each other. There was Yacov Rambsel (2005), Zola Levitt (2006), David Allen Lewis (2007), Ray Brubaker of *God's News Behind the News* (2009), David Wilkerson (2011), J. R. Church (2011), Hilton Sutton (2012), Grant Jeffery (2012), Jack Kinsella (2013), Dave Hunt (2013), Charles Pack (2014), Steve Hill (2014), John Paul Jackson (2015), and a noted voice in charismatic circles, Kim Clement (2016). This does not include gifted pastors or evangelists who loved to teach biblical prophetic truth. There are others carrying the weight of responsibility to proclaim end-time prophetic messages, but the voices are becoming fewer with each passing year.

I believe the silence of the prophetic voices is a visible gauge that God is withdrawing his face of favor from our nation. After years of warnings, with no turning from wickedness, God will eventually give up on a people, turning them over to reprobate minds and own choices without his intervention (see Romans 1). Biblically, any judgment cycle is preceded first with a call to repentance, followed by a season of mercy, often mixed with ominous dreams, visions, and vocal warnings given to the righteous for necessary preparation. When warnings cease, voices are still, and prophecies are mocked; eventually a regional, national, or global judgment has been sealed. Lot's sons-in-law mocked him only hours before balls of fire from heaven fell, scorching the perverse city of Sodom. Sodom's influence was stronger than Lot's warning, causing Lot's other family members, along with several of Lot's daughters, to miss their moment of escape. Once so-called "righteous" individuals become mockers, there is no more extension of mercy, only judgment (see Genesis 19).

Often in Israel, one lonely man cried out against Israel and Judah's iniquities. Labeled as negative fanatics, these prophets were often forced into isolation by decree of rebellious kings and angry priests. Jeremiah was the lone-ranger prophet, blaring out warnings to his generation of Jerusalem's future Babylonian destruction. His reward for his warnings was being lowered into a miry pit, separating him from the masses he irritated with the tone and tenor of his warnings (see Jeremiah 38). The prophet Micaiah was also secluded in a dungeon when he was taken out to give a "word from God" to Ahab. He was the only true voice among an echo of 400 false prophets, all of whom were under the spell of a lying spirit (see 2 Chronicles 18:22). Micaiah was willing to confront King Ahab, predicting his upcoming death in battle, but he was slapped in the face by another "prophet" with an opposing "word." Micaiah was right, and the other false prophet was wrong. Elijah alone challenged the government leaders of his time while other "prophets" hid in caves for security to prevent their premature death by the hands of Queen Jezebel (1 Kings 18:4; 19:18). John the Baptist was a single "voice in the wilderness" crying out against injustice and religious hypocrisy. His outspoken style led to his imprisonment and his beheading by Herod, whom John had rebuked for an "illegal marriage" (Mark 6:24-29). Paul penned fourteen letters to believers throughout the Roman Empire. At the conclusion of his ministry in Rome, Paul was beheaded on Nero's chopping block, falsely accused of starting a fire that burned 70 percent of Rome's Circus Maximus. Paul wrote that "all men forsook me" (2 Timothy 4:16), indicating that Christians in the Roman Empire believed a lie—that Paul instigated the fire in Rome—when in reality Paul was the scapegoat Nero used to cover his own actions for burning Rome. These examples illustrate that true prophets are never popular with those in political, and at times spiritual, authority.

God's authentic prophets are not riding in plush Rolls-Royces or savoring morsels of expensive caviar with a tiny silver spoon in the cities' most expensive restaurants. They are not pimping out their limited-edition sport vehicle for a month's long vacation. The honest, pure-hearted, and sincere prophetic men and women I have encountered are usually the ones being lambasted on social media, mocked by their own denominations as "too radical," and only have a faithful remnant attending their meetings. They have never, nor will ever, be invited to a "seeker-sensitive" convention.

When King Saul, Israel's first king, grieved God, disobeying his divine mandate, the Spirit of God departed from the stubborn king, leaving him unprotected and vulnerable to his adversaries. When God's Spirit departed from Saul, an evil spirit took up residence in him (1 Samuel 16:14). The Lord refused to communicate with Saul by dream, vision, or the priestly Urim and Thummim. Saul's sad life concluded after he sought out a witch and, the following day, fell on his own sword in his final battle (1 Samuel 31). Saul proved that once the voice of God is silenced, the door to failure and demise is opened.

WHOSE VOICE IS THAT?

Contrary to advocates of the theological argument of cessation, God has never not spoken in some form from Adam to the present. He continually speaks, but often his people have waxed ears, calloused hearts, or dull spirits. In the time of Samuel, not only was there no "open vision" from God, but also, when God did speak, Eli the high priest was so far detached from God's presence that he was impotent in determining whose voice was speaking to the child Samuel. Eli and the boy Samuel were sleeping in the same room, yet Eli heard nothing when the boy was hearing an audible voice. In Eli's day the tabernacle of Moses was in Shiloh, but rituals had replaced the Word of God as "the word of the Lord was precious in those days" (1 Samuel 3:1). The Hebrew word *precious* here means "valuable" or "rare." The spoken word from God was rare, and the priesthood was so corrupt that the shady ministers at the tabernacle could no longer perceive God's voice. The tabernacle rituals went uninterrupted, but the presence of God went missing. And sadly, God's presence was never missed by the priests.

In the days of Samuel, Israel had no king, and the people did what they felt was "right in their own eyes" (Judges 17:6). The Law of Moses was copied on scrolls for priests and elders to instruct the people, but self-rule and personal opinions toward what was actually right and wrong prevailed over God's Word. Judges had been raised up, authorized by the Lord to deliver Israel from internal and external enemies. However, once the people were freed from their enemy's captivity, the chains of bondage began rattling again as the people, over time, found themselves in the same repetitive cycle of complacency and idolatry. In the time of Samuel, the spiritual corruption had infected the priesthood, as the sons of Eli the high priest, Hophni and Phinehas, were accepting bribes, abusing sacrifices, and committing fornication with women at the very entrance to Moses' tabernacle (see 1 Samuel chapters 1-4).

The nation was so far removed from the light of God's Spirit that the Lord severed his communication lines with the priests, instead choosing to reveal his intimate plans to a young child named Samuel. Eli refused to discipline his evil sons for their numerous sins, which caused God to rebuke them, calling them the "sons of Belial," a name meaning "worthless."

One of the first signs in ancient Israel that God was displeased with his people was when he turned them over to a bad leader and did not restrain that leader from making bad decisions that negatively impacted the entire nation. Solomon's son, Rehoboam, is an example. After Solomon's death, this son became king. He refused to hear the older people, instead listing to advice from unwise and unseasoned youth. His decisions led to Israel being divided between ten northern tribes (the northern kingdom) and two southern tribes (the southern kingdom).

A second prophetic parallel from Samuel's time mirroring our generation is found in 1 Samuel 3:3: "And ere the lamp of God went out in the temple of the LORD, where the ark of God was, and Samuel was laid down to sleep."

The lamp here refers to the menorah, a golden candelabra that was to remain lit at all times and whose oil was to be replenished daily and "burn always" (Exodus 27:20). Without the light from this candlestick, it became impossible for a priest to burn the daily incense or minister in the holy place. Without the light, the priests were "ministering in the dark." The horrible spiritual condition of Eli was also significant, as we read "his eyes were dim," meaning he had very poor natural vision. Poor vision is a spiritual metaphor for the inability to properly discern spiritual matters (Isaiah 42:17-20). With the priest's eyes dim, they could not tell if the light in the holy place was bright, dim, or darkened, as his own eyes were partially blinded. The top of the Temple menorah had seven lamps, and these lamps were in the form of eyes, representing the eyes of the Lord, continually observing activities in the sacred chamber. When believers become dull of hearing and dull of seeing, we will lose our ability to hear God's voice or discern the voice we are hearing.

3.

THE SIGN OF AMERICA'S FUTURE SHAKING

AMERICA WILL "SHAKE"

Years ago, on August 23, 2011, a 5.8 earthquake struck the east coast with its epicenter near the town of Mineral, Virginia. Oddly, according to the United States Geological Survey, this quake was felt in twelve states by more people than any other quake in United States history. Geologists point out that because of the rock strata in the east, an eastern quake can be felt over an area ten times larger than on the west coast.

The quake also shook Washington, D.C., damaging two nationally recognized structures: the Washington Monument and the National Cathedral. The majority of Christians would consider this mild quake a natural fender-bender that held little significance since no lives were lost. However, at the National Cathedral, three of the four corner spires on the Cathedral's center tower crashed to the ground, costing millions of dollars to repair. Cracks appeared on the top of the famed Washington Monument—150 in all. Oddly, the quake occurred 150 years from the beginning of the Civil War that divided the nation (April 12, 1861 to August 23, 2011). The monument, the world's tallest stone structure, required being shut down and repaired. Using some discernment as to what these two structures represent, the cathedral symbolizes America's religious faith, and the monument is a memorial to the founder of our nation. Thus, using these buildings as a prophetic imagery of the nation, the "religion" and "foundational truths" were shaken. And since the natural is a reflection of the spiritual, our religious and historical foundations in America are being challenged, shaken, and changed by progressives in high places.

THE JERUSALEM EARTHQUAKE

King Uzziah was a beloved king of Judah who ruled in the days of the prophets Amos and Isaiah. According to Amos 1:1, a major earthquake rattled Jerusalem and Judea in the days of Uzziah. Modern geologists found evidence confirming this earthquake after examining the ground strata in six ancient cities excavated by archeologists. Geologists dated this quake to the eighth century B.C. and believe it registered between a 7.8 to an 8.2. It was so horrific, its violent force jolted stone columns, crashing them to the ground in the lower areas. This earthquake created a noted and recently confirmed (by a Tel Aviv geological group) major fault line stretching across the Mount of Olives in Jerusalem. It's the same fault line the prophet Zechariah predicted would give way when the Lord returns to earth (Zechariah 14:4). Today, there are hundreds of acres of land on the Mount of Olives where no building has been, or will be, constructed, as it would be foolish to build a home, church, or business on this fault line. Years ago, a major hotel chain desired to purchase this portion of property and build a beautiful tourist hotel whose rooms would face the Eastern Gate and the Temple Mount. After geological research and testing, they declined after finding that the ground underneath was unstable.

It should be noted that King Uzziah, while a good leader most of his life, willfully broke the divine order of God by entering the Temple as a king and offering incense at the golden altar. It was a sacred ritual reserved only for the Levites and the priesthood (see 2 Chronicles 26). The king became angry for being reprimanded, and while the incense censor was in his hand, God struck him with leprosy, a disease he endured until his death (2 Chronicles 26:20-23).

There are two types of earthquakes in the Bible. One type occurs, but no one is killed. Examples are when Elijah was on Mount Horeb with God, when Christ was crucified and raised from the dead, and the earthquake that destroyed the prison, releasing Paul, Silas, and others from their cells (1 Kings 19:12; Matthew 27:54; Matthew 28:2; Acts 16:26). In these examples the earthquakes were sent as a sign from God, yet no lives were taken since this was not an act of judgment but a sign of God's power. The second type of earthquake, however, is a sign from God—a warning or an act of judgment. Biblically, when these occur, there can be a loss of life, as observed in the Apocalypse when in the future tribulation another earthquake will rattle Jerusalem, taking out one-tenth of the city (Revelation 11:13). The greatest earthquake in world history is set to occur in the second half of the great tribulation, when the cities of the nations will collapse. John said it will be an earthquake unlike any that has ever occurred on the earth (Revelation 16:18).

King Uzziah dishonored the law of God, and as a result, the mountains trembled in Judea, and the ground quivered throughout Israel. Was the D.C. earthquake just a rare freak of nature that has no significance? Or was it a "sign" that there were "cracks" coming in America's politics (the monument) and in our religious faith (the cathedral)? Since 1912 the National Cathedral has been called the "spiritual home for our nation in the time of crisis." The Washington Monument is a marble obelisk towering over Washington, D.C., to honor George Washington as our first president and his work on America's independence. The cornerstone was laid on July 4, 1848, exactly 100 years before Israel would be reestablished as a nation. The monument is 555 feet, five and one-eighth inches high, which translates to 6,666 one-eighth inches. The foundation goes down 111 feet below the ground, and from the ground to the top is 555 feet, making a total of 666 feet. 666 is the number of mankind and also the number connected with the coming Antichrist (Revelation 13:18). In Revelation 13:18, this number can prophetically allude to men controlling the governments of the world.

WHAT INTERCESSORS SAW

Oddly, a small prayer group knew several months prior that a physical shaking would occur in Washington, D.C. Amos 3:7 states that God will do nothing unless he "first reveals his secret to his servants the prophets." This would include both male and female believers whose ears are in tune to God's voice. In May 2011, one of our youth named Lauren was praying in our OCI prayer barn with about thirty others, interceding for the nation. Suddenly she experienced an open vision, which she later revealed to us and recorded in her journal. Here is part of her journal entry:

> "I saw a shaking come to Washington, D.C.—both in the spiritual and natural. When I was looking at the map it was a shaking that shot out in four directions— north, south, east, and west. A shaking will completely shake the political realm . . ."

There is more insight from the political arena I will leave out. She then continued to write and speak: "I feel a huge literal earthquake is coming that shakes and changes the east coast. Then I saw a new president rise."

We do not believe that the August 2011 quake is the "big one" coming on the east, but it is the original shaking she saw in the first part of the vision. The "big one" is still in the future, but will most definitely impact the nation's capital.

TORAH PORTIONS AND NATIONAL DISASTERS

For centuries now, it has been customary for all Jewish synagogues throughout the world to read the same passages of Scripture every week. The preselected passages, taken from the Torah and the Prophets, are called *parasha* and *haftarah* respectively. Amazingly, there are times when the weekly Torah reading will correspond in a prophetic way with current events that unfold in Israel and throughout the world. When this occurs, it is often viewed as a word from the Lord God. He is speaking to the world through his Word to offer edification, exhortation, comfort, and warning.

Consider this very interesting example. Just days before Barack Obama was first sworn in as the forty-fourth president of the United States on January 20, 2009, the parasha that was being read around the world was *Shemot*. In English, this word means "names" and is actually the Hebrew name given to the book we call Exodus. That particular parasha begins in Exodus 1:1 and ends with Exodus 6:1 and this statement: "Now you shall see what I will do to Pharaoh." It is also within that Torah portion that the Bible tells us that after the death of Joseph and that generation, "there arose a new king over Egypt who did not know Joseph" (Exodus 1:8).

Observing this verse and other information that came to my attention, I predicted then that President Obama would not be friendly toward Israel during his administration. Bill Cloud and I then began noting the different points written in the Exodus narrative that described a crafty and hostile pharaoh whose disdain for the Hebrews led to the implementation of policies designed to enslave them. It was amazing and alarming to see how these different policies paralleled those initiated by the Obama administration. It became obvious very early on that the president's opinion and attitude toward Israel and, for that matter, God's people at large, was not a favorable one.

On more than one occasion, Obama refused to meet with Israel's Prime Minister Benjamin Netanyahu and, according to multiple news sources, showed great contempt for Netanyahu in conversations with other world leaders. The brutal fact is, Obama has proven to be the least friendly of any U.S. president to Israel since she became a nation in 1948. This is in spite of the fact that he boasts of being the friendliest. Furthermore, there have been times when he and his administration actually supported Israel's enemies such as Hamas, Hezbollah, and Iran. It is important to note that this same ill feeling toward Israel goes beyond the tiny Middle Eastern nation. In other words, this same contempt has been directed at those in this country who stand with Israel and, more importantly, call upon the God of Israel! So then, is it possible that the Torah portion being read in the days leading up to Obama's inauguration were God's subtle way of alerting us to what is going on? I would also like to point out that, upon the occasion of Obama's trip to Cairo in June 2009, he was greeted by Egyptians as the "new Tutankhamon of the world."

It is interesting to note the Torah reading the week before the D.C. earthquake. The Torah reading was taken from Deuteronomy 7:12 through 11:25 and included a stern warning to God's people who break his laws. In fact, God reminds them to learn from their past by calling attention to their sin with the golden calf—a transgression so great that 3,000 died in one day. It is also in this section that Moses reminds them of the two tablets of "stone" that were broken because of their disobedience (see Deuteronomy 9:11-17).

But on the day of the earthquake, the parasha being read was, in Hebrew, *Re'eh,* which literally means, "See!" It's as if to say, "Look at what happens when you don't obey my voice." That portion begins with the statement, "Behold (see) I set before you today a blessing and a curse," and it goes on to admonish God's people when they enter Canaan to "destroy their altars, break their sacred pillars and burn their wooden images with fire" (Deuteronomy 12:3). I'd like to call your attention to the Hebrew term translated as "pillars." The word *matzebah* means a "memorial stone." In other words, this term describes an upright memorial made from stone that was dedicated to something or someone to be worshipped other than the Almighty.

The cracks that appeared in both the Washington Monument and the National Cathedral were not at the foundation as one might expect, but instead at the top of the structures, the highest points. Both buildings are constructed of stone, and in the case of the Washington Monument, it is fair to say that it qualifies as an upright pillar dedicated to the veneration of a man. I might also add that this particular monument is modeled after an Egyptian obelisk! While there is nothing wrong with acknowledging people who display virtue and godly character, let us remember that God chose to bury Moses secretly so that his people would not be drawn to the gravesite of so great a man. He knew that, in time, it would become an object to be venerated. Case and point: later in the time of King Hezekiah, the brazen serpent that was used to save so many in the wilderness had to be destroyed because it had become an object of worship (2 Kings 18:4).

So could it be that the Torah portions can hint at, or even warn, of such events? Do these parashot give us insight into what is going on in our day? And why would God use this method to speak to Americans? Before a person writes this off as fanciful and/or the wild imagination of a prophetic minister, consider that the earthquake occurred on the 400-year anniversary of the translation of the 1611 *King James Bible*. It is a matter of fact that most American presidents have used a King James translation of the Bible when being sworn in. Thus, the earthquake occurred during the 400th anniversary of the most popular translation of the world's most beloved book, the Bible. It's a covenantal book whose principles this nation adopted as their own. Consequently, we shouldn't be surprised if God uses the principles in this book to speak to us in ways that are obvious to those who are paying attention. This "coincidence" is important to point out because 400 is a significant number in Scripture. Specifically, it is the number of years God told Abraham that his descendants (Israel) would be sojourners in a land that was not their own. This four-century period would terminate when God would bring his people out from Egypt and into their promised land (Genesis 15:13). Consequently, the nation of Egypt—once the greatest power on earth—would collapse and never be the same again.

There are other intriguing elements of the Washington quake that might allude to biblical or prophetic parallels. For instance, the epicenter of the quake was in Mineral, Virginia, eighty-four miles from Washington. The seven-year tribulation, a time when the world will be shaken as never before, is a total of eighty-four months (seven twelve-month years). As I said, the foundation of the damaged buildings was not affected, but it was the top of these buildings that were cracked. Throughout Jerusalem's history, when the walls of the city were breached by enemies, it was almost always the top stones of the walls that were toppled, leaving the stone foundation intact. In the case of Jerusalem, the foundation is actually the mountain upon which it was built; this is especially true when it comes to the Temple Mount—a mountain called Mount Moriah. When Solomon built God's house, the bedrock of Moriah was cut into stone formations so that the first row of stones to be set were placed upon the mountain itself, making the foundation unshakable. Today, despite numerous earthquakes, Jerusalem's foundation remains as a testimony that God favors Jerusalem.

On the other hand, the fact that the walls have been top-pled and breached multiple times is testimony that God will bring correction to a nation that abandons his Word. The foundation our nation was built upon is embedded with biblical principles—chief among them is that there is a God in heaven who raises up and brings down nations. Since our founding, however, other things have been built that steer us away from God and his Word. Often, those things that represent our waywardness are tall structures men love to venerate.

Shortly after 9/11, I was ministering in Baton Rouge, Louisiana, at Healing Place Church. It was there where I met a young Jewish girl who had been employed at the World Trade Center but who was not in the building when the planes struck. She felt impressed to present me with three papers. On one side of one paper there were Scrip-tures from Isaiah written in Hebrew and English. On the other side, she had written her personal observations and emotions about what she saw and experienced that day. She recounted the awful dusty smell and the presence of death and horror. Of the passages from Isaiah she had highlighted the following verses that seemed to hold an ee-rily cryptic message when considering the events of 9/11. The passages read:

> "The burden of the wilderness of the sea. As whirlwinds in the South sweep-ing on, it cometh from the wilderness, from a dreadful land. A grievous vision is declared unto me: the treacherous deal-er dealeth treacherously, and the spoiler spoileth. Go up Elam, besiege oh Me-dia. All the sighing I have made to cease.

Therefore my loins are filled with con-
vulsion: pangs have taken hold upon me,
as the pangs of a woman in travail: I am
bent so that I cannot hear; I am affright-
ed so that I cannot see. My heart is be-
wildered, terror has overwhelmed me . . .
arise ye princes anoint the shield" (Isaiah
21:1-5).

In an English Bible, the heading for Isaiah 21 makes
clear that this is an address to Babylon (modern Iraq). Of
course, this is one of two primary areas in which the war
on terror would unfold after 9/11. We know that all nineteen hijackers were Muslim, many of whom had links to
Saudi Arabia, the cradle of Islam and a land that is situated south of Israel. In these passages the prophet spoke of
"fearfulness," but it could be better translated as "terror."
As we know, striking terror into the hearts of Americans
was the goal of those who conceived and carried out the
attack. The word "whirlwinds" certainly describes the
scene the world witnessed when the towers collapsed and
sent gray dust funnels into the air and the streets of lower Manhattan, blinding everyone in their path. When the
towers collapsed, the noise was so deafening people could
not hear.

The nations of Elam and Media, those that "went
up," would include Iran, which borders Afghanistan, the
very place the instigator of the 9/11 attacks, Osama Bin
Laden, made his base of operations. Fear most definitely struck our nation and overwhelmed all who personally
saw the attack in the manner Isaiah describes. The en-
suing instruction in Isaiah was for princes to "anoint the
shield," meaning they were to get ready for battle. Under

President George W. Bush, the United States took the war to the enemy.

Since the numbers in Scripture have meanings and often prophetic events are centered around specific numbers or time frames, it is interesting to note that this D.C. earthquake occurred on the 235th day of the 235th year anniversary of America's independence. Perhaps a coincidence—but interesting nonetheless.

ANOTHER JUBILEE PREDICTION

Rabbi Judah Ben Samuel was a Regensburg German Hassidic rabbi from the thirteenth century who became noted for his predictions about Jerusalem and the coming Messiah. Christian clerics even sought out his wisdom and advice. When once asked where he received his wisdom, he claimed that Elijah the prophet had appeared to him and revealed certain events involving the future.

At age fifty-five the rabbi wrote two important books. The first was lost, but the second book exists. Both books were written at the time crusaders were in possession of the Holy Land. The second book, written about 1270 A.D., predicted that Palestine would fall into the hands of the Muslims. Rabbi Samuel went as far as to predict that the Turks would control Jerusalem in the future: "When the Ottoman (Turks) conquer Jerusalem they will rule over Jerusalem for eight jubilees. Afterwards, Jerusalem will become a no-man's land for one jubilee, and then in the ninth jubilee it will once again come back into the possession of the Jewish nation, which would signify the beginning of the Messianic end time."[5]

In Leviticus 25, a Jubilee cycle is derived by counting seven years seven times, or forty-nine years. The fiftieth

year becomes the jubilee, whose theme is liberty and redemption and includes a provision to restore land that was
sold back to the original owner. Three hundred years after
the rabbi's writing, in 1517, the Turks seized Palestine and
Jerusalem. It was the Turks who initiated a reconstruc-
tion project for the walls of Jerusalem, building the upper
section that can be seen today. This was the fulfillment
of Isaiah's prophecy over Jerusalem: "The sons of strangers shall build up your walls" (Isaiah 60:10). The word
"stranger" in Hebrew means a foreigner. Isaiah also wrote
that Jerusalem's "gates would be opened continually" (Isaiah 60:10). Today all gates in Jerusalem are continually
opened with the exception of the eastern gate, which has
been sealed for hundreds of years.

The rabbi also alludes to Turkish rule continuing for
eight jubilees, which would be fifty multiplied eight times,
or 400 years. Oddly, it was at the conclusion of eight jubilees that the British armies, under the leadership of General Allenby, liberated Palestine, entering Jerusalem on
Hanukkah, December 17, 1917. Hanukkah is the yearly
festival of "lights" commemorating the Jewish revolt that
liberated Jerusalem and the Temple from the Greeks. Jerusalem experienced a second prophetic liberation that
day placing Palestine and Jerusalem into Christian hands,
exactly at the conclusion of 400 years (1517–1917), or
eight jubilees.

The amazing prediction of "no man's land" for one
jubilee is extremely interesting. In 1917 Jerusalem was divided between the Jordanian and British, with a large concrete wall stretching through the middle of the city and
military posts watching the "other side." This was actually
called No-Man's Land, and the wall could not be claimed
land by either side. This situation changed in June 1967

following the Six Day War when Israel united the east and west sections under their control, removing the concrete separation barrier and allowing free movement for its citizens and tourists throughout the city. The No-Man's Land border block was torn down after fifty years—or one jubilee—in 1967.

Following this stunning transition, the next prediction given by the rabbi is the tenth jubilee (1967 to 2017), signaling the Messianic era. 1967 to 2017 completes fifty years, or the tenth jubilee cycle. Having traveled to Israel over thirty-four times in the past thirty years, I have observed the change in attitude among Jews toward Christians. I believe this tenth jubilee cycle may indicate a uniting of "one new man" under the Messiah and a coming revival that will spread globally into all nations (Joel 2:28-29).

HARBINGERS LINKED TO ISRAEL

A harbinger is a person, thing, or sign that signals the approach of something else. They are often called "signs" of the time of the end by Bible scholars. Signs are events that foreshadow a future event predicted in the Bible. The restoration of modern Israel was not just a harbinger but a fulfillment of Bible expectations for the time of the end.

1ST HARBINGER—ISRAEL WOULD FACE NEAR EXTINCTION BEFORE RETURNING TO THE LAND

In Ezekiel's vision of the valley of dry bones (Ezekiel 37), the question is asked, "Can these bones live?" (Ezekiel 37:3). In this vision something terrible has happened to the "whole house of Israel" (Ezekiel 37:11), as they are described as being in "graves" with no breath remaining in them. Their bones cry out, "Our bones are dried, and our hope is lost; we are cut off from our parts" (Ezekiel 37:11). This "cutting off" can certainly refer to entire families that were cut off from one another during the seven-year Holocaust. With six million Jews (1.5 million children) dying in the Holocaust, one-third of the world's Jewish population was exterminated, and had the allies not gone to war with Hitler, there would have been millions more deaths. Thus, Israel would face near extinction before returning to the land. The Ezekiel vision (chapter 37) has not been fulfilled as there is no historical evidence where the details of Ezekiel's dry bones vision ever occurred. When the allies entered the death camps, the precious survivors were barely alive and starving. They looked like skeletons covered with skin, a visual imagery similar to Ezekiel's dry bones prophecy.

2ND HARBINGER—ISRAEL WOULD BE REBORN IN ONE DAY

The United Nations decreed a Jewish homeland on November 29, 1947, yet, considering the new location was in Arab territory called Palestine that already existed, fulfilling this decree required a political process from leading nations to pursue the name, location, and government to create a nation that did not exist. It would be months later, in May 1948, when the British Mandate over Palestine ended at midnight, forcing the British to give up their occupation of Palestine and allowing an invisible nation to become visible, all in one day. In fact, one second after the British Mandate concluded at midnight May 14, 1948, Israel was officially a Jewish state. This brings to mind the ancient narrative that in Egypt at midnight, the Egyptians lost control over the Hebrew slaves, and at the same time, at midnight, Israel was prepared for a great exodus to their land (Exodus 11:4). That night one nation (Egypt) declined in authority, and another (Israel) rose to power.

Isaiah foretold this time when he wrote, "Who hath heard such a thing? Who hath seen such things? Shall the earth be made to bring forth in one day? Or shall a nation be born at once? For as soon as Zion travailed, she brought forth her children" (Isaiah 66:8). The phrase "bring forth" in a day is the Hebrew word *chuwl* and means "to wrist or whirl" and also to "dance in pain." This is interesting as the rebirth of Israel was through the "travail" (birth pangs) of the Jews following the Holocaust; thus, there was rejoicing, yet in pain. There was joy for those survivors given a homeland and pain when remembering the suffering and deaths of millions who would never live to see this day.

3ʳᴰ HARBINGER—ISRAEL WOULD BE ONE NATION AND NOT DIVIDED INTO TWO NATIONS

This prediction, found in Ezekiel 37:21-22, indicates that when the people of Israel return to their land, the nation would be united as one and not divided as it was in the days of the Hebrew prophets. From the time Jacob's sons return under Joshua until the days of King Solomon's son, Rehoboam, Israel was one united nation. Eventually, Israel became divided between the two northern and two southern tribes, or the northern and southern kingdoms.

Ezekiel said that God would "join them one to another into one stick; and they shall become one in thine hand" (Ezekiel 37:17). Ezekiel said, "I will make them one nation in the land upon the mountains of Israel . . . they shall no more be two nations, neither shall they be divided into two nations; neither shall they be divided into two king-doms any more" (Ezekiel 37:22-23). Today, there are no tribal divisions as Israel is one nation.

4ᵀᴴ HARBINGER—ISRAEL'S (THE JEWS') RETURN WOULD BE GREATER THAN THE EXODUS

Before 1948, this prediction seemed quite an embel-lishment, and how it would occur was hotly debated or glossed over by theologians. It was not alluded to, or in some instances, was marked as a passage to be fulfilled at the return of Christ when the angels would "gather his elect from the four winds of heaven," re-gathering the Jewish elect from the north, south, east, and west (Mat-thew 24:31). Take a careful look at an amazing prediction given by the prophet Jeremiah:

> "'Therefore behold, the days are com-ing,'" says the LORD, "that it shall no more be said, "The LORD lives who brought up the children of Israel from the land of Egypt," but, "The LORD lives who brought up the children of Israel from the land of the north and from all the lands where He had driven them." For I will bring them back into their land which I gave to their fathers'" (Jeremiah 16:14-15 (NKJV)).

To prove that this verse does not refer to angels gath-ering the Jewish people at the end for the tribulation, note the following explanation of "how" this return would oc-cur. The Lord said, "I will send many fishers . . . and they shall fish for them; and afterwards I will send my hunters, and they shall hunt for them from every mountain and every hill (Jeremiah 16:16). These "fishers" and "hunters" are metaphors for men or organizations who would assist in discovering the location of the Jews and organize transportation bringing them back. Numerous Christian and Jewish organizations have assisted in transporting Russian Jews and Jews from the "north" back to Israel. Today there are tens of thousands of Russian-speaking Jews who are living and working in Israel. The return of the Jews from Gentile nations is not just a millennial prophecy—it has been occurring and continues to occur now!

5ᴛʜ Harbinger—Israel Would Rebuild Old Cities and the Land Would Prosper

Upon Israel's return, there would be years of rebuilding the waste places. Amos penned this when he said:

> "And I will bring again the captivity of my people of Israel, and they shall build the waste cities, and inhabit them; and they shall plant vineyards, and drink the wine thereof; they shall also make gardens, and eat the fruit of them. And I will plant them upon their land, and they shall no more be pulled up out of their land which I have given them, saith the LORD thy God" (Amos 9:14-15).

I have personally watched this verse come to pass during numerous pilgrimages to Israel. Notice the blessing on the land follows the Jewish "captivity." This was partially fulfilled when the Jews returned to Judea from Babylonian captivity. However, the prophet speaks of "Israel" and not just Judea. Israel is the land promised to Abraham; thus, its main fulfillment would be after 1948, when farms began dotting the barren wilderness. Also, when the devastated cities are rebuilt, and the vineyard and fruit trees are planted, "they shall no more be pulled up out of their land." This cannot be the exiles after Babylon, as 656 years later, the Roman Tenth Legion destroyed Jerusalem, forcing the Jews from their land. In this passage, once the Jews return, they will not be "pulled up," a phrase from the Hebrew word *nathash*, meaning to "tear away and root up," indicating a physical removing of the people.

The land will become so productive that the plowman would overtake the reaper (Amos 9:13), indicating more than one harvest a year, which is now occurring in the Jordan Valley where hundreds of farms are harvesting every type of vegetable and fruit imaginable.

6ᵀᴴ HARBINGER—ISRAEL WOULD REBUILD A STRONG (GREAT) ARMY WHEN THEY RETURN

In the days of the Babylonians and Romans, swords and spears were the two common weapons provided to armies in all nations. When Jews revolted in the days of the Greek enemy Antiochus Epiphanies, basic weapons were used in their revolt that lasted for forty-two months, eventually wearing down the Greeks. In the years prior to the Roman destruction of Jerusalem, Jewish rebels would unite men with a promise they could defeat the Roman occupiers, only to suffer violent deaths or arrest and public punishment. Israel did not have any organized and armed army to defend themselves.

When Israel is restored, Ezekiel notes that they will become a "great army." We read, "they lived and stood up upon their feet, an exceeding great army" (Ezekiel 37:10). The word "exceeding" in Hebrew is *me'od* and can refer to speed and quickness, which accurately describes Israel's army today. The Hebrew word "great" here is *gadowl*, and means great in any sense—in size, in sight, in ability—indicating this will be an undefeatable military force.

Israel has fought surrounding nations in wars: 1947-49 War of Independence, the Suez War with Egypt in 1956, the Six Day War in June 1967, the Yom Kippur War in 1973, the Palestinian Uprising in Lebanon in 1982, and the Lebanon war with Hezbolah in 2006. Many other minor wars originating with Hamas in Gaza and numerous intifadas with Palestinians have erupted off and on for years. However, in the major wars, Israel has come out victorious, with the exception of 2006 when they restrained their bombing objectives since women and children were being used as human shields. Today, Israel has perhaps the fourth most powerful military in the world. It is not their size but their technology and stunning air force that is secretly feared by enemy nations.

7ᵀᴴ HARBINGER—ISRAEL WOULD FILL THE WORLD WITH FRUIT GROWN IN ISRAEL

Part of Israel's GNP comes through income derived from the sale of produce, including some of the most delicious fruit grown anywhere in the world. Isaiah foresaw Israel's future agricultural impact when he wrote, "Israel shall blossom and fill the face of the world with fruit" (Isaiah 27:6). The Hebrew word for fruit in Isaiah 27:6 is *tenuw-*

bah, basically meaning produce of any type that is grown. It is from the Hebrew root word *nuwb*, alluding to germination and causing to flourish. In 1948, much of the land partitioned for Israel was a swamp or a dry desert, in which not much would grow. David Ben-Gurion, Israel's first prime minister, was an avid lover of the desert and set his heart on helping the desert become a productive part of Israel.

Today, Israel produces 95 percent of its own food requirements, importing sugar, coffee, cocoa, meat, and some grains. Much of Israel lacks water for irrigation. However, underground sources were discovered near Qumran off the northern edge of the Dead Sea and in the Arabah, below the Dead Sea, being tapped into for farm use, thus enabling the arid desert to "blossom like a rose" (see Isaiah 35:1-7). More than forty types of fruit are grown in Israel, and researchers have developed a variety of foods, such as a special tomato that grows in the desert region. In Jericho, Jerusalem, and major Israeli cities, outdoor markets are crowded with shoppers selecting some of the finest fruits and vegetables grown anywhere in the world. Millions of tourists make pilgrimage to Israel each year, awakening at sunrise to enjoy a huge Israeli buffet breakfast of tasty and healthy fresh produce grown in Israel's once-arid deserts, now thousands of farms. These farms stretch from the Galilee in the north to the Dead Sea in the south.

When the desert blossoms and produces fruit, the prophet Isaiah wrote that the "excellency of Carmel" would be given to it. In Israel, one of the international fruit producers is Carmel Agrexco, an international fresh fruit brand name that helps with agricultural technology and fruit production.[6] Isaiah spoke of Israel's deserts "filling the world with fruit," which was impossible in his day for three reasons. First, the land was basically desert with little rain or water sources. Second, there was a method (such as refrigeration) to get the fruits and food "around the world," and third, Israel was a nation that at times could barely feed its own people, much less those in other nations. To early rabbis, one sign of the age of the Messiah would be when the land of Israel would bear food and fruit. This is now occurring throughout Israel.

8ᵀᴴ HARBINGER—ISRAEL WOULD RETURN FROM GENTILE NATIONS ONCE AND FOR ALL

The biblical prophet Micah was made aware by the Spirit of God that the remnant of Israel would dwell among the Gentiles: "And the remnant of Jacob shall be among the Gentiles, in the midst of many peoples, like a lion among the beasts of the forest, like a young lion among flocks of sheep, who, if he passes through, both treads down and tears in pieces, and none can deliver" (Micah 5:8).

The prophet Hosea added this prophetic commentary: "Israel is swallowed up; now they are among the Gentiles like a vessel in which is no pleasure" (Hosea 8:8). The time would come when the Jewish people would no longer feel safe or content dwelling in Gentile lands. Moses said:

> "Then the LORD will scatter you among all peoples, from one end of the earth to the other, and there you shall serve other gods, which neither you nor your fathers have known—wood and stone. And among those nations you shall find no rest, nor shall the sole of your foot have a resting

place; but there the LORD will give you a
trembling heart, failing eyes, and anguish
of soul" (Deuteronomy 28:64-66).

The Jews throughout history have been the most harassed and persecuted of any ethnic group. There are 109
locations, towns, cities, and nations where Jews have been
expelled since 250 A.D. Even in the United States, in the
days of President Ulysses Grant, the president issued an
order refusing permits for Jews to come south for cotton
sales. As he said in his letter to the assistant adjutant general of the U.S. Army, Jews were violating regulations of
trade.[7] From 70 A.D. to today, had the world's Jewish population been warmly accepted in every nation, never been
persecuted, and thrived in business, there is little possibility they would have left their Middle Eastern and European homes and businesses, making exodus to Palestine
or Israel after 1948. Following the Holocaust, having lost
their homes, lands, possessions, and bank accounts, there
was nowhere for most survivors to turn but toward the
Holy Land or friendly Western nations willing to take in
Jewish refugees. The yoke of Gentile dominion, however,
would one day be broken from the necks of the Jewish
people—a time and seasons noted in Scripture as "the
fullness of the times of the Gentiles."

Christ himself drew attention to the fact of Gentile
dominion and control over Jerusalem being shattered in
the future: "And they will fall by the edge of the sword,
and be led away captive into all nations. And Jerusalem
will be trampled by Gentiles until the times of the Gentiles are fulfilled" (Luke 21:24). From the time of the Babylonian invasion, Jerusalem became the city of political
conflict and Gentile armies. Beginning with the Greeks,

below is a list of the years and the Gentile powers that throughout history dominated nations in the Middle East and had direct dealing with the Jews or direct control of Jerusalem.

- 333 B.C. to 63 B.C. – The Greeks dominated the region
- 63 B.C. to 313 A.D. – The Romans dominated the region
- 313 to 636 A.D. – The Byzantines dominated the region
- 636 to 1099 A.D. – The Arabs and Muslims dominated the region
- 1099 to 1291 A.D. – The Crusaders dominated the region
- 1291 to 1516 A.D. – The Mamelukes dominated the region
- 1517 to 1917 A.D. – The Ottoman Turks dominated the region
- 1917 to 1948 A.D. – The British dominated the region

From 70 A.D. to 1948, Abraham's promised land was under Gentile possession—controlled by Gentile monarchs, kings, governors, and leaders. Two Gentile empires forced the Jews from their homeland into exile: the Babylonians and the Romans. It is interesting that Jewish rabbinical commentaries link the Romans as the descendants of Esau, and Rome is often identified with the name Edom in rabbinical literature, especially in the days of Roman oppression against the Jews. Two major dispersions from the land were predicted, and the biblical seers saw the people uprooted from the peace and security of their homes but also noted how the Jews would survive in Gentile lands. They would eventually return at a set time to rebuild their homes in Israel. The Babylonian Exile centered in Babylon, but the Roman Exile scattered the Jews globally. Yet when the appointed time came for their return, the Jews were re-gathered, rebuilt, and prospered in their land. The disciples understood this return and its connection to the kingdom of God and asked Christ, "Will you at this time restore the kingdom to Israel?" Christ answered that it was not for them to know the times and seasons that God alone controlled (Acts 1:6-8). There would be a divine appointment set on God's calendar bringing the Jews out of Gentile land as Psalm 102 indicated. God would favor Zion, and the "set time" to favor her has come (Psalm 102:13). In the Psalm 102:13 passage the Hebrew word for "set time" is *mowed*, the singular Hebrew word used for a festival or convocation in Israel. The seven festivals in the Torah are called the *moadim*, plural for "appointed times." God has set his times for prophetic events, and we are living in those prophetic times and seasons (Acts 1:7; 1 Thessalonians 5:1).

9TH HARBINGER—THE JEWS SHALL RETURN TO THE LAND BY FLYING LIKE CLOUDS

In an amazing prediction, Isaiah revealed the method used by returning to Israel at the end of days: "Who are these that fly as a cloud, and as the doves to their windows? Surely the isles shall wait for me, and the ships of Tarshish first, to bring thy sons from far, their silver and their gold with them, unto the name of the Lord thy God, and to the Holy One of Israel, because he hath glorified thee" (Isaiah 60:8-9).

Jews began making Aliya to Israel in large numbers beginning in 1948. The word *Aliya* means "ascent" and is used when Jews outside of Israel return to their Jewish homeland. Since 1948, over 3 million Jews have returned to Israel from Gentile lands. When Jews began returning to Israel in 1948, many made their journey on ships to Palestine. However, sixty-two of the sixty-three immigration ships carrying mostly Holocaust survivors were turned away by a British blockade at the port of Haifa. During the past seventy years, the mode of transportation for new immigrants has changed from ships to planes, with hundreds of thousands of Jews permanently departing from former Gentile homelands, including over 1 million Russian Jews taking permanent root in Israel. Isaiah predicted they would "fly," comparing their return to moving "clouds." Clouds float through the upper atmosphere, move in "bunches," and move with increased speed as the wind blows. It's a perfect analogy of people flying in groups on a plane "in" the clouds.

Isaiah twice noted this method of "flying" when he also wrote: "But they shall fly upon the shoulders of the Philistines toward the west" (Isaiah 11:14). The word "fly" in this verse in Hebrew is the same word used when birds fly (Genesis 1:20), when cherubs fly through the air (2 Samuel 22:11), and when a dove flies (Psalm 55:6). Thus, the word "fly" is not a *metaphor* but *literal*. People flying is mentioned four times in the Old Testament (Isaiah 11:14, 60:8; Jeremiah 49:22; Habakkuk 1:8). Reading these verses, Sir Isaac Newton predicted that, in the future, the Jews would return to Palestine by flying in the air. Newton was mocked by noted infidel Voltaire, who criticized Newton for his belief that one day men would fly. Isaiah, in the eighth century B.C., about 2,700 years before air transportation, predicted the Jews would "fly on the shoulders of the Philistines." The ancient Philistines once controlled the coastal areas of Israel, from Gaza in the south to present-day Lod in the north. The following paragraph sums up the amazing prediction of Isaiah: The term "ketef Philistia" is a geographical landmark where the hills of Shephela end over the valley of Ajalon. Across the valley is the ancient Lydia or Lod. It is situated upon the shoulders of the ancient Philistines. Ben-Gurion Airport is there, and all Jews returning to Israel fly there!

Every Jewish immigrant returning to Israel by airplane "flies" to one main airport: the Ben-Gurion Airport in Tel Aviv. The Jews emigrating from the North Country, such as Russia, must all fly to Israel, landing in the ancient geographical area of the "shoulders of the Philistines." Recently, in one year alone 16.3 million passengers flew in or out of this airport. Built in 1936 during the British Mandate for Palestine, Israel took possession in 1948 when Jews began flying back to the newly formed state of Israel.

In the New Testament, the word "fly" is mentioned three times, all in Revelation: 12:14, 14:6, and 19:17. Twice the word is used in connection with an angel who will fly in the sky and proclaim two messages: one, a message of the gospel (Revelation 14:6); the other refers to a call for flesh-eating birds to assemble to eat the flesh of men at the battle of Armageddon (Revelation 19:17). In Revelation 14:6, an angel is proclaiming the gospel from the air. Some prophecy teachers suggest this "messenger" could refer to a satellite in the upper atmosphere that will continue bringing the gospel through modern communication methods during the tribulation. Inspired by this passage, one of America's faith-centered Christian and family networks is called Skyangel, which operates three television networks on the DISH satellite platform. The third reference to "fly" is in Revelation 12:14, referring to the "woman" (Israel) given two wings like an eagle to fly into the wilderness. This prediction could be more than some metaphor, but it may imply that a Jewish remnant will be transported by air to a secure location for forty-two months, away from the armies of the Antichrist. In the Old and New Testament eras, the very thought of people flying like birds would have been ridiculed. However, today we can see and understand this possibility through air transportation, and the Jews are returning home on the shoulders of the ancient Philistines' territory.

10TH HARBINGER—ALIGNMENT OF NATIONS IN ISRAEL'S TWO PROPHETIC WARS

Two of Israel's most significant future wars are the Gog of Magog battle detailed in Ezekiel chapters 38 and 39 and the mother of all battles identified by the prophetic title, The Battle of Armageddon (Revelation 16:16). In the time of the prophets, war weapons were bows, arrows, spears, swords, and soldiers riding on horseback or in chariots. In the biblical war prophecies, there is a possibility that the prophets who viewed these end-time battles also saw advanced weapons or military machinery, which they attempted to describe with their limited understanding, requiring an updated interpretation in our time, as prophetic knowledge would be increased at the time of the end (Daniel 12:4). An example of a different interpretation is how some rabbis point to Psalm 2:9, relating the words to a cryptic reference to missiles: "Thou shalt break them with a rod of iron; thou shalt dash them in pieces like a potter's vessel" (Psalms 2:9).

In apocalyptic literature, when Christ returns he will destroy his enemies with the "sword of his mouth," a metaphor for the power of his spoken words (Revelation 2:27; 12:5; 19:15). The "rod of iron" phrase is also a metaphor used to describe the kingly rule of the Messiah when he returns to rule the nations "with a rod of iron" or exercising firm control over all people and nations. However, the "rod of iron" in Psalm 2:9 has been interpreted by some rabbis as concealing a double reference, alluding to missiles or rockets made of metal ("iron") that have been for modern warfare fired from rocket launchers into Israel, attempting to break the strength of the Jewish people, thus "dashing them like a potter's vessel." These "rods of iron" or missiles have broken through concrete buildings, exploded on the land, split rocks, and, at times, taken innocent lives.

Some have gone as far as to stretch a similar interpretation to the "flying roll" seen and described by Zechariah and penned in Zechariah 5:1-2: "Then I turned, and lifted up mine eyes, and looked, and behold a flying roll. And he said unto me, What do you see? And I answered, I see a flying roll; the length thereof is twenty cubits, and the breadth thereof ten cubits."

The Hebrew word "roll" here is *megillah*, which is a scroll similar to a Torah scroll, shaped like two small tubes. The megillah is one of the five biblical books—Song of Solomon, Ruth, Lamentations, Ecclesiastes, and Esther—that are read on certain festivals and sacred days. The Zechariah roll is seen by the prophet flying in the air and is twenty cubits by ten cubits or an estimated thirty-three feet long by eighteen feet wide, using the standard Hebrew cubit of one cubit being eighteen inches long. However, for a modern missile, the Zechariah measurements of the width of the roll does not equate with the roll's length, as a modern missile with this disproportionate size would be aeronautically unable to fly. In an attempt to make this missile imagery fit, some prophetic teachers point out that this "flying roll" consumes a house with wicked people by destroying the timber and the stones (Zechariah 5:4). However, in the text, this flying roll is a curse and not a missile. In this Zechariah reference, it is best to keep the text as a literal scroll with writing on the parchment that is sent to its destination with the assistance of angelic messengers (see Zechariah 5).

There is a war reference in Jeremiah whose warnings of the Babylonian invasion were ignored for several decades. In the final chapters of Jeremiah, the prophet describes the seizure of Jerusalem and lists the Temple treasures seized from Solomon's Temple and carted away as war spoil back to Babylon (Jeremiah 51 and 52): "Make bright the arrows; gather the shields: the LORD hath raised up the spirit of the kings of the Medes: for his device is against Babylon, to destroy it; because it is the vengeance of the LORD, the vengeance of his temple" (Jeremiah 51:11).

Ancient armies in Jeremiah's time did not use "bright" (flaming) arrows in battle. These were first used by the Persians in 480 B.C. who invaded Greece using fiery projectiles to burn down the Greeks' man-made wooden barricades surrounding temples. The Greeks later tapped into this burning projectile strategy fifty years later, and the Romans also pulled burning arrows out of their arsenal against adversaries. The Babylonian invasion of which Jeremiah speaks was over 100 years prior to the use of fiery arrows. So what were these burning arrows?

This has generated a rabbinical thought that possibly

the "bright arrows" allusion may be a prophetic "double reference," not to a metaphor related to fires set at Jerusalem by the Babylonians, but may conceal a *prophetic code* predicting future wars in the Babylonian region today known as Iraq. This interpretation was presented to me by a Jewish rabbi from Hungary who was flying beside me on our way back to the states after preaching in Romania prior to the Gulf War. He believed these "bright arrows," historically, were never used by ancient Babylonians but were actually modern missiles, about to be released in the Iraqi war. When striking their targets, these missiles blew objects to pieces, creating bright fires. The trails left by missiles could look like the tail of a comet or falling star to an ancient mind who saw a prophetic vision and was unaware of future modern weaponry. After carefully looking at the Jeremiah reference, the rabbi's insight is interesting to say the least, as in both Iraqi wars (occurring on the land of ancient Babylon), the night sky lit up like daylight when U.S. missiles exploded on their targets.

A DEDUCTION MADE FROM A WAR VERSE

There are times when a biblical prophecy may not express a direct statement, but when examining the context with specific words, there is an *implied meaning* that expands the interpretation of that verse. One such example is found in Ezekiel's Gog of Magog war, in which troops from Meshech, Tubal, Persia (Iran), Libya, Ethiopia, Gomer, and Togarmah unite against Israel in an epic, latter-day war (Ezekiel 38:1-6). This organized coalition of Israel's enemies consists mostly of Islamic nations who swiftly descend like a "cloud" covering the northern mountains in Israel and also swarming like bees on the eastern mountains located east of the Dead Sea. The northern location is identified by Ezekiel as the "Bashan," also known today as the Golan Heights (Deuteronomy 4:43; Ezekiel 39:18), with a second war front on the east of the Dead Sea near the Valley of the Passengers (Ezekiel 39:11), a large mountain range located east of the Jordan River northeast of the Dead Sea, overlooking the Jordan Valley and Jericho. Oddly, the highest point of this region is Mount Nebo, where Moses viewed the promised land prior to his death. In ancient times a road ran through this area called "The King's Way" (Numbers 20:17,19). Ezekiel describes this two-pronged battle erupting on the "Mountains of Israel" (38:8; 39:2; 39:4; 39:17). It was this area of Moab where Balak paid Balaam to curse Israel (Numbers 22-23). This same area was annexed by the tribes of Reuben and Gad. Jacob gave a prophetic word concerning Gad: "A troop will overcome him; but he will overcome in the last" (Genesis 49:19). The Hebrew word "troop" here is *geduwd*, meaning "a crowd, especially of soldiers." Could this prophecy about Gad refer to the armies attacking Israel in this ancient tribal region during the Gog of Magog war, that will temporarily appear to overcome this area, yet Israel will overcome in the "last?" The Hebrew word "last" is used thirty-two times in the Old Testament and is the Hebrew word *'achariyth*. It refers to the future—the latter time and the end. However, this Hebrew word "last" in the Gad prediction in Genesis 49:19 is *'aqeb*, the Hebrew root word in the name Jacob (Ya'aqob). This Hebrew word means "heel." The imagery is that Israel will put its enemies under its heel, a metaphor for a great victory for Israel and a crushing defeat for its enemies.

The Valley of the Passengers alluded to in the Ezekiel war vision lies between two mountain ranges in Jordan on the east side of the Jordan River, in the nation of Jordan, which shared a border with Israel. However, the Golan Heights or Bashan from 1948 through 1967 was land belonging to Syria. During the 1967 war, Syria lost this region to Israel and has since made numerous political attempts, including an October 1973 counter-war on Israel's Yom Kippur (Day of Atonement), to regain the northern land lost in 1967. The "prophetic implication" in Ezekiel's battle sequence is that Israel will be in complete control of all the Bashan when Ezekiel's Gog of Magog war erupts. Currently, the mountains in northern Israel are called "the mountains of Israel" and not just "the Bashan." If these mountains in the Golan Heights, which were once southwestern Syria, were today under Syrian control, there would be no necessity of these Islamic enemies invading "Israel" to "take a spoil" (Ezekiel 38:13). The "deduction" from this passage is that Israel will be in control of the Golan Heights (the Bashan) when this prophetic battle occurs. Israel seized the Golan toward the end of the 1967 war, capturing thousands of acres of rugged land covered with mines and concrete bunkers surrounded by barbed wire. This area is also the fresh water source for Israel, and the southern half is fertile farming land as forty-one Israeli settlements are in the Golan Heights.

Again, using deductive reasoning, the premise in Ezekiel would indicate that the war of Gog of Magog could *not have occurred* as long as Syria possessed the Golan Heights, as the invaders listed in the text are not Jews in Israel attacking the Syrians, but outside Islamic nations organizing a massive host with armed troops covering the mountains of Israel. Thus, the minute details of this battle could not have unfolded until Israel was a nation

(1948) and gained possession of this ancient biblical territory called the Golan and the Bashan in 1967. This indicated the year 1967 became a pivotal prophetic year of alignment, paving the path for future prophecies to follow the road of fulfillment. Notice the order of Ezekiel's visions: first the dry bones live again and form a great army in Israel (Ezekiel 37), and the following two chapters (38 and 39) expose Israel's enemies plotting and participating in an invasion, when Israel is dwelling safe and at rest in un-walled villages (Ezekiel 38:11). This describes Israel's present living conditions: cities without walls. The bones of the house of Israel are living again, Israel has become a great army securing the land, and today it is surrounded by many hostile nations, including one nation that desires Israel's destruction, Iran, known as the ancient Persians.

THE KINGS OF PERSIA AND ARABIA

An 800-year-old rabbinical prophecy found in the Yaluk Shimoni, a compilation of rabbinic commentary on the Bible dating to the thirteenth century, states that when the king of Persia provokes the king of Arabia, redemption is around the corner. Persia is today Iran, and Arabia is Saudi Arabia; both are Islamic nations. However, the general population and governments of these two nations differ in their religious beliefs and interpretations, as the Persians are predominantly Shia Muslims and the Saudis are Sunni Muslims. These two groups have been warring among themselves since the death of Mohammad. Saudi has been under threat from the mullahs in Persia (Iran) for years, which has resulted in Saudi maintaining close ties with Britain and America for economic reasons (oil), military protection, and the needed intelligence information required to prevent a hostile overthrow of the "house of Saud" from Islamic radicals and the armies of the Persians.

This has also caused Saudi Arabia to conduct negotiations behind the scenes with Israel, as Israel has discussed for years an attack on Iran's nuclear bunkers and facilities where Iranian scientists are researching both nuclear and biological programs in secret locations within the Persian mountains. This attack would require flying over Saudi airspace, which has been negotiated in private negotiations, as both the Saudis and Israelis view the Shia religious leaders in Iran as future threats to their security.

11ᵀᴴ HARBINGER—NATIONS PRAYING IN JERUSALEM

If any other world religion, outside of Christianity or Judaism, were in possession of Israel and Jerusalem, Jews and Christians would be forbidden to pray publicly at the Holy places, and some religions would even ban Muslims from attending prayer at the mosques. Because Israel allows religious freedom to all people, millions are permitted to publicly pray in Jerusalem at a famous stone wall called the Western Wall, an outer retaining wall of large stones that survived the Roman destruction in 70 A.D.

King Solomon, Israel's third king, spent nearly seven years constructing the most expensive and elaborate temple in world history, estimated by some to be worth $140 billion in today's economy. It was made of gold, silver, wood, and other costs. His magnificent dedicatory prayer was recorded by a scribe and placed in the biblical archives. In the prayer, Solomon stepped into the role of a seer predicting strangers (KJV), or foreigners (NKJV) who would make their way to Jerusalem for prayer:

"Moreover, concerning a foreigner, who is not of your people Israel, but has come from a far country for the sake of Your great name and Your mighty hand and Your outstretched arm, when they come and pray in this temple; then hear from heaven Your dwelling place, and do according to all for which the foreigner calls to You, that all peoples of the earth may know Your name and fear You, as do Your people Israel, and that they may know that this temple which I have built is called by Your name" (2 Chronicles 6:32-33 (NKJV)).

In reality, it was predominantly Jews both in Israel and scattered throughout Gentile nations who came to the Temple for the festivals and for prayer. The second temple ceased to exist in 70 A.D., and no Jewish house of prayer has been constructed on the previous site of the first and second temples. However, this wall and its plaza in Jerusalem has served as a place of prayer for both Jews and people of all nations.

In the days when the red heifer was offered (Numbers 19), worshippers would pray from the Mount of Olives facing the eastern doors of the Temple. After Jerusalem's destruction and the later construction of two Islamic mosques on the Temple Mount, the freedom for Jews and Christians to pray on the sacred mountain was either limited or restrained. In fact, in the early 1990s, I was reading from the Bible on the Temple Mount and was removed by guards who said that only a Quran could be read in their holy site. The same has been true with prayer. Muslims are permitted to pray, but non-Muslim praying is stopped. At times, when Jews were spotted praying on the Mount, riots broke out, and the site was closed to tourists.

The famous Western Wall was a retaining wall constructed by Herod the Great to hold tons of dirt when he expanded the Temple platform, extending it to the south. When the Turks took Jerusalem in 1517, much of this wall was concealed with tons of garbage: the spot was considered the "trash dump" for inhabitants in and around Jerusalem. It was believed that the Romans began this tradition, bringing garbage and dumping it in this spot so the name of Israel would be erased. In the sixteenth century, during the rule of Sultan Suleiman the Magnificent, a woman from Bethlehem was bringing her garbage, dropping it in this location. After hearing her explain why, the Sultan began throwing coins in the trash heap for the poor to dig and discover. News spread as the poor assembled, removing layers of rubbish for thirty days, as he added coins from time to time to inspire them to continue the digging process. Eventually, the entire area was cleared, exposing the now-famous Western Wall and a plaza. A rabbi, recalling the decision of the Sultan, pointed out a verse in Psalms. The KJV reads, "He raiseth up the poor out of the dust, and lifteth the needy out of the dunghill" (Psalm 113:7). The rabbi interpreted this verse this way: "He raises up the needy from the earth and he lifts up the poor from the garbage heap."

The exposed area was used for public prayer. The wall is 187 feet long and faces a large plaza with the height of the exposed section being sixty-two feet. There are forty-five stone courses with twenty-eight above ground. These large limestone ashlars have a chiseled border, forming a hands-breadth frame. The large stones weigh between two and eight short tons and are set on top of one another in a manner to prevent the upper wall from toppling in the event of an earthquake.[8]

Each year, upwards of ten million people visit the Western Wall from all nations, united by individual prayer at one holy location. Reviving an old tradition when the wall was liberated in 1967, a tradition begun by General Moshe Dayan at the end of the Six Day War is to place a small written prayer request on paper in the cracks of the wall. Millions of individuals—Jewish and Christian—make pilgrimages to Jerusalem, and the majority visit and pray at the Western Wall. Solomon spoke of a "foreigner" coming to pray. These would-be non-Jewish believers traveling to Israel from Gentile nations, which would include the 4 to 5 million Gentile tourists visiting Israel each year.

From May 1948 to May 1967, the Western Wall was actually under the oversight and control of Jordan, along with ancient Judea and Samaria, Bethlehem, and Jericho. In early days, there are photographs of Jews standing at the wall praying; however, once Jordan took possession of the area, no Jews prayed there. Near the time of 1967 King Hussein of Jordan had discussed building a five-star, resort-type hotel, making the Western Wall the interior of the hotel. Before the first plans could be drawn, the Six Day War erupted, and the Western Wall became the possession of Israel.

The stones of Jerusalem have a prophetic role. The first sign of the *beginning of the end* of Jerusalem in 70 A.D. was when the Temple stones were toppled and not one stone was left upon another (Matthew 24:2). The first sign of the last days prior to the Messiah's return would be a restoration of the walls, gates, and the city of Jerusalem, including the former Temple areas as multitudes will travel to Jerusalem for prayer.

For Solomon's prayer to be answered and his prediction of "foreigners" praying at the Temple to be fulfilled in the last days, *Israel must be in control* of Jerusalem and this place of prayer. The Western Wall is the closest Jews can pray near the site of the previous two Jewish temples, which were both built on top of the hill of Moriah. The first massive prayer event for Jews to occur at the wall was when Jerusalem was "liberated" on the third day of the Six Day War, as over 200,000 Israelis poured in from west Jerusalem to the ancient wall, some spending hours and others entire days celebrating, praying, and in awe. Since 1967, strangers (Gentiles) pray continually at the place where the former house of God once stood, fulfilling Solomon's prediction.

12ᵀᴴ HARBINGER—THE PROPHETIC STONE

In Psalm 102, the inspired psalmist speaks of a "set time" when God will favor Zion (Jerusalem). He speaks of how God's servants "take pleasure in the stones" of the city (Psalm 102:14). The stones on the Western Wall are called in Hebrew the *kotel*, meaning "wall." In the year 66 A.D. the Romans first surrounded Jerusalem with the final destruction happening in 70 A.D. Almost nineteen centuries ago, these rectangular and square-shaped hand-cut ashlars of limestone rock, once stacked proudly on Jerusalem's wall, lay in massive piles along the base of the western side of Jerusalem's wall, a silent witness of Christ's warning in Matthew 24:1-3. When the massive Roman "engines" hit solid limestone rocks head on, forcing them from their secure resting place, tons of broken ashlars came crashing to the ground like a crumbling stone mountain. They were too large to move and remained for eighteen centuries exactly where they were, hidden from human sight as layers of dirt and numerous occupations of Jerusalem covered the evidence of the Roman invasion. Following the Six Day War, Israeli archeologists began a series of excavations, exposing Jerusalem's history and removing the debris, observing the ruins exactly as they were the day Jerusalem's walls were breached.

It was 1,900 years after this destruction when a stone that is part of the original wall was unearthed, measuring nine feet above the ground. Carved directly on the surface of the stone, in Hebrew, was a verse found in Isaiah 66:14: "When ye see this, your heart shall rejoice, and your bones shall flourish like an herb." The person who etched this verse was unknown, and archeologists suggested it was carved perhaps as late as the third century by a Jew anticipating the eventual hope of Israel's restoration that Isaiah predicted for Israel: "Who hath heard such a thing? Who hath seen such things? Shall the earth be made to bring forth in one day? Or shall a nation be born at once? For as soon as Zion travailed, she brought forth her children" (Isaiah 66:8).

Isaiah is alluding to the restoration of Israel as a nation, which would occur in a day and suddenly at once. The Scripture on this stone, now called "The Rejoicing Stone," was concealed as this area was under Jordanian control until after June 1967 and was exposed by Dr. Benjamin Mazar, when Israel took control of all of Jerusalem.

The stones referencing "bones rejoicing" is quite interesting and refers back to Ezekiel's vision of dry bones, where God "breathes upon the bones," and they live (Ezekiel 37:5-6). The inscription reads, "When you see this," implying that it would be concealed for a long period and then emerge for eyes to see. This inscription was on this stone for centuries but never seen as debris concealed it. Then, after the Holocaust (1945), Israel was rebirthed as a nation (1948), and soon after, Jerusalem was reunited as the capital of Israel (1967). It was shortly after Jerusalem was reunited and under Jewish control that this amazing stone was exposed for all to see.

This stone is today found on the western side of the wall, above ancient ruins of massive stones toppled in 70 A.D. by the Romans. It is not considered a part of the prayer court of the Western Wall. Since devout Jews cannot freely pray on the Tempe Mount with two Islamic mosques and Muslims claiming the entire mount site for their religion, the Western Wall is the main prayer area in Jerusalem for Christians and Jews. In earlier times, Jews would hammer a nail on the wall as a symbol for a good journey, based upon a word in Isaiah 22:23: "I will fasten him like a nail in a sure place."

The following verse, found in the Song of Solomon, is said to prophetically refer to the Western Wall as "behind" the "wall." It is a reference to the Temple Mount where Jewish temples once rang out with music and the sound of worshippers.

> "My beloved is like a gazelle or a young stag.
> Behold, he stands behind our wall;
> He is looking through the windows,
> Gazing through the lattice.
> My beloved spoke, and said to me:
> 'Rise up, my love, my fair one,
> And come away'" (Song of Songs 2:9-10).

It is noted that the Hebrew word here for "wall" is

different than translated in other Old Testament passages. The word is *kotel*, a word used for a compact wall like the Western Wall, and the name Jews give the Western Wall today is the kotel! Here, God is standing behind the wall looking at his beloved, bidding them to come away with him (through prayer).

All types of prayers are offered continually by both Jews and Gentiles standing at the wall. Christ once spoke a unique promise related to his return when he said, "For I say to you, you shall see Me no more till you say, 'Blessed is He who comes in the name of the Lord!'" (Matthew 23:39, (NKJV)).

This phrase is originally found in Psalm 118:26. In Psalm 118:25 we see the psalmist saying "hosanna," meaning "save now." The *na* suffix on the word *hosanna* in the Hebrew expression of this word denotes intense emotion. This word, *hosanna*, was the cry of worshipers when Christ rode on a donkey into the Temple (Matthew 21:9) as the multitudes were hoping Christ would be crowned King of Israel, delivering the Jews from their Roman oppressors. This same prayer of "blessing the one who is coming (the Messiah)" is offered today at the Western Wall at various seasons by devout Jews who believe the arrival of the Messiah is imminent.

13TH HARBINGER—1948 ENCODED IN THE GENEALOGIES

I have shown these phenomenal charts in several previous articles and books I have written, but they bear repeating in the context of the significance of 1948 in association with Israel's supernatural restoration. Often, biblical readers question why the Holy Spirit would inspire a biblical writer to list the *years* of specific events, especially when found in a long genealogy, which is a list naming the ancestors emerging in a family lineage. For example, when writing the Torah, Moses began with Adam and noted he was 130 years of age when his third son was born to Eve (Genesis 5:3). Moses then proceeds forward in history to name the year when each man's first son was born, in the order of their birth from Adam to Abraham. From a Western theological thought, the names are important to follow the lineage to Abraham, but there is no "logical and significant reason" for giving their age at their first son's birth. From a rabbinical consideration of this enigma, the rabbis believe there is at times a "concealed" reason for alleged mysteries in Scripture. Perhaps this is one of them.

Below is a list of names and numbers, beginning in Genesis 5 and continuing through Genesis 11, that give the order of the sons born through Adam to Abraham, noting the age of each man at his firstborn son's birth. Notice what occurs when we add up the numbers in this genealogy—the first set being from Adam to Noah, and the first ten men in history before the flood:

THE NUMBERS OF ADAM TO NOAH IN GENESIS 5

- Adam was 130 when Seth was born (Genesis 5:3)
- Seth was 105 when Enos was born (Genesis 5:6)
- Enos was 90 when Cainan was born (Genesis 5:9)
- Cainan was 70 when Mahalaleel was born (Genesis 5:12)
- Mahalaleel was 65 when Jared was born (Genesis 5:15)
- Jared was 162 when Enoch was born (Genesis 5:18)

- Enoch was 65 when Methuselah was born (Genesis 5:21)
- Methuselah was 187 when Lamech was born (Genesis 5:25)
- Lamech was 182 when Noah was born (Genesis 5:28)
- Noah was 500 when his sons were born (Genesis 5:32)

1,556 total years listed

The following numbers recorded in Genesis 11, after the flood, are listed from Shem (Noah's sons) to Abraham:

- Shem was 100 when Arphaxad was born (Genesis 11:10)
- 2 years after the flood (Genesis 11:10)
- Arphaxad was 35 when Salah was born (Genesis 11:12)
- Salah was 30 when Eber was born (Genesis 11:14)
- Eber was 34 when Peleg was born (Genesis 11:16)
- Peleg was 30 when Reu was born (Genesis 11:18)
- Reu was 32 when Serug was born (Genesis 11:20)
- Serug was 30 when Nahor was born (Genesis 11:22)
- Nahor was 29 when Terah was born (Genesis 11:24)
- Terah was 70 when Abraham was born (Genesis 11:26)

392 years

When adding the years 1,556 and 392, the total number of years from Adam to Abraham totals 1,948 years. This number is prophetically significant for this reason. Christ is identified in 1 Corinthians 15:45 as the "last Adam," a term indicating his parallel with the first Adam and how Christ regained, through his death, what the first Adam lost during his life, eternal life. If we begin counting years from the zero year—which marks the calendar change linked with Christ's birth, marked in the Christian calendar as A.D.—moving forward to the year the natural seed of Abraham officially was recognized among the nations and returned back to their promised land, Israel, the date occurred 1,948 years after the "zero year," marking Christian time.

These harbingers, spiritual signs, or as some call end-time prodigies have all occurred since the year 1948. They are the foreshadowing of the main prophetic events that will eventually lead to the return of the Messiah, Jesus Christ, to set up his kingdom on earth for one thousand years (Revelation 20:1-4).

4.

AMERICA, WHAT HAPPENS WHEN GOD STOPS WARNING US?

"The Revelation of Jesus Christ, which God gave unto him, to show unto his servant's things which must shortly come to pass; and he sent and signified it by his angel unto his servant John"
- Revelation 1:1

The book of Revelation was inked on parchment near or shortly after the year 95 A.D., meaning this apocalyptic vision is presently over 1,900 years old. It is from the moment the apostle John was seized in a spiritual trance, piercing the veil of tomorrow to declare future events. The one phrase that has occasionally initiated debate has been John's phrase, "things which must shortly come to pass." After nineteen centuries of history with the Antichrist not yet rising or seven-year tribulation yet to be unleashed, did John misspeak by saying the things he saw would come to pass "shortly?" Some groups, identified as preterists, interpret this phrase of "shortly coming to pass" to mean "came to pass in the first century." However, the Greek word for "shortly" is a preposition that can refer to a time being swift, or quick. In the context, John is saying that once these events begin to unfold on earth, they will move very quickly and swiftly; from one judgment to the next, and one scene in the Apocalypse to the next.

Noah presents an example of the swiftness in which a word from God can be fulfilled. Noah was given 120 years to prepare the ark after being warned a deluge was coming (Genesis 6:3). Nothing significant occurred for 120 years except for Noah's ship-building program, which finally finished when he was six hundred years old. When every detail was complete, God waited seven days before sending the rain (Genesis 7:4). Without warning, the underground waters erupted as torrents of rain plummeted to the ground for forty days, lifting the floating houseboat with eight souls and a zoo full of animals above the mountains. Notice that the earth's population did not perceive what was coming until the actual day the flood judgment arrived (see Matthew 24:38-39). This is the pattern with all historic judgment cycles. There is a warning, followed by a season of grace and mercy. At times a second warning is announced, accompanied by a brief "space to repent" (Revelation 2:21). Finally, the one set day arrives, and as Israel learned, the Babylonians are at your front door, or the Roman legion has breached the gates of your city.

REACTIONS TO PROPHETIC WARNINGS

Warnings of impending danger, judgment, and coming calamities were given to Israel through Moses, Isaiah, Jeremiah, Daniel, Ezekiel, and numerous other prophets. These words still remain part of the Old Testament cannon. In the New Testament, Christ, Paul, Peter, and the apostle John spoke significant insights revealing future events—some that would occur within their generation, such as the destruction of the Temple (Matthew 24:1-3) and others to be fulfilled in the far future, experienced by generations not yet born.

It is not just the warnings but the *reaction* to the warnings that are noted in Scripture as there were two opposing reactions: one was *rejection* of the prophet and his words, and the other was *repentance* and *humility* resulting from a fear of the Lord's anger and possible judgment. Six thousand years of history proves these two opposing reactions have been the factors determining whether God releases judgment or mercy. The Assyrian city of Nineveh was given a forty-day mandate to repent, or destruction would be released (see Jonah). The leaders and people chose humility over pride and repentance over arrogance, and the city was spared for an additional 150 or so years. Another example is Christ's trial before his death sentence. The religious hierarchy was given two options: release Jesus, an "innocent" prophet and teacher, or crucify this "innocent" man, releasing a blood curse upon the people. With audacious arrogance the religious crowd consisting of a majority of Torah-observant Jews announced a self-curse: "His blood be upon us and upon our children" (Matthew 27:25). Nineveh was given forty days to turn or burn, but Jerusalem was given forty years, or one generation, 480 months, to turn from their unbelief. Still, they chose their own future, breaking a serious law of shedding innocent blood (see Deuteronomy 19:10-13).

I was born in Parsons, West Virginia, June 23, 1959. In 1977, at age eighteen, I began traveling on the east coast in several states preaching revivals in local churches. My simple ministry grew from rural congregations to an international outreach, with our messages being heard weekly in hundreds of nations globally. However, my strongest burden continues to be for America, as I often ponder where we will end up as a nation. Through the years when the Holy Spirit would give me what I call "right now" prophetic messages, I would observe five common reactions from Christians sitting in the average American church. These particular five responses are the wrong ones that need to be exposed and corrected.

FIVE WRONG REACTIONS FROM BELIEVERS

The first wrong reaction from believers is to apply every word of warning only to America. In the nineteenth century, the British were made aware of Bible prophecy through British ministers emphasizing and writing about what the prophetic Scriptures revealed concerning future events. In the twentieth and twenty-first centuries, America saw the raising up of numerous prophetic scholars and teachers taking center stage, causing the sheep to become spiritually "fat" and overloaded with information from prophetic insights, proving this generation is in the time of the end, advancing toward Christ's return. This prophetic information explosion can be accredited to Christian authors exposing their messages in bestselling books, Christian movies emphasizing apocalyptic themes, and Christian television expanding the gospel message to almost every home in North America.

Because of this "prophetic overload," it is common when a vision, dream, or prophetic warning is released, for Christians in the West to first apply the warning or the blessing mainly to North America or discuss how it will impact America. Biblical warnings, though, are for the *entire world* and not just one nation. We must have a worldview of prophecy and not a North American exclusionist theology. This is important considering that in biblical apocalyptic literature, the East, South, and North are alluded to, but the West is strangely missing, or the Bible is silent with no direct reference to the western hemisphere.

The second is to believe the word will immediately take place. In June of 1996 I experienced a clear, full-color vision of the World Trade Center shrouded in total black with five greyish colored spinning tornados, emitting dust. Sparks were flying off the building. I knew this was a warning of something terrible occurring in the future at the Trade Center. However, nothing significant occurred year after year to indicate the fulfillment of the vision until five years later, on September 11, 2001, planes flew into the Trade Centers. One of the common mistakes believers make is to hear a true prophetic warning and think that it will *immediately* come to pass, and if it doesn't, over time, they tend to "blow it off" and soon forget what was seen in the Spirit or spoken. There is a spiritual principle in Revelation 2:21 that God presents a warning but does not immediately respond in judgment. God said he gives a "space to repent," meaning a set time in which grace is extended prior to the Lord lifting his mercy and allowing the judgment.

There are verses written two and three thousand years ago by prophets whose holy bodies have long returned to dust, yet by faith we know their foretelling of coming events are accurate and will ring true in time. Warnings precede the events, and the gap between the judgment cycle and warning may be extended by God who is long-suffering and not willing that any perish (2 Peter 3:9).

The third mistake is to place dates on what is not dated. Over the years, one of the common blunders among prophecy teachers and ministers is to make numerical calculations announcing a particular year or specific calendar date in which the Lord will return, the Antichrist will be revealed, or the tribulation will begin. In my lifetime I heard Jesus would come in 1973 (following the Yom Kippur War) and then in 1982 because of alleged "alignment of planets" expected to bring global destruction. This was followed by "88 reasons Christ would return in 1988," a forecast which of course proved incorrect. In 1991, the Gulf War, a Middle Eastern conflict in the heart of ancient Babylon, created a prophetic sensation with some suggesting Saddam was the Antichrist, and this conflict would initiate the beginning of the end. Eight years later, the Y2K band wagon was beating its drum to the tune of a global economic collapse at one second after midnight, January 1, when computers' internal clocks rolled over. With each highly anticipated event, a specific calendar date was marked that passed without the return of Christ.

Attempting to set days or hours for Christ's return based on newspaper exegesis or tying a major event into a vague prediction causes the predictor to end up red-faced with humiliation, bringing embarrassment to the ministry and confusion in the body of Christ. The most negative comments emerge from unbelievers who are already convinced that prophetic students are a bowl of fruits and nuts, at the least. If Christ and the angels are unaware of the day and hour of his return (Matthew 24:36), then God would not disclose this age-old mystery to any mortal man. Tell the warning, the dream, or vision, but omit specific date-setting.

A fourth mistake is to despise what has been spoken or mock it. In the mid 1980s around 1984, I learned about an excavation for the last ashes of a red heifer offered on the Mount of Olives in Jerusalem. One Hebrew scholar believed it was hidden in the Qumran area. After future research and studying this sacrifice recorded in Numbers 19, I discovered that devout Jews, who strictly follow the ritual and sacrificial regulations in the Torah, would require these ancient ashes or burn a new red heifer's ashes for ritual purification, in the event a future temple would be constructed in Jerusalem. I began to preach a noted prophetic update message simply titled, "The Ashes of the Red Heifer."

In those days during my extended revivals, Saturday night was noted as a "prophecy update night" where I preached, illustrating my evidence using color slides from Israel. The churches were often packed with believers and non-believers, both interested in end-time subjects and how events tied into Scripture. However, I can recall the severe mocking, ridicule, and criticism I received from my own denominational ministers who did not understand the message or the purpose of its content. It was years later when one minister who was my worse skeptic on the subject heard a rabbi in Jerusalem explain the necessity of the "ashes of a red heifer" for temple purification. Later, this minister stood on a tour bus in Israel and apologized to his church members for making fun of my message on the ashes of the red heifer. Shortly thereafter, in about 1988, *Time* magazine featured an article on the rebuilding of the third temple and alluded to the need for the ashes of the red heifer for ritual purification. It further authenticated the information I had been sharing for four years. It took the secular, in the eyes of many, to confirm what I had been teaching all along.

Peter warned that scoffers would mock the message of Christ's return in the last days (2 Peter 3:3). We should judge things not by what we think we know but from what Scripture and the facts clearly reveal. And if we are skeptical, we should do deeper research before making a final judgment on a prophetic message that is new to us.

The last wrong reaction from believers is to think God cannot speak to simple people. In Matthew 2, the Magi arrived at Herod's palace notifying the ignorant king of a cosmic star sign and its link to the birth of a new Jewish king. Herod inquired of the scribes and Pharisees as to where the future Jewish King-Messiah should be born. These devout Jewish scholars agreed on the location. They all said, "Bethlehem." However, notice that not one scribe, Pharisee, or administrative representative associated with Herod walked across a few rugged hills or rode a horse six miles to Bethlehem to visit this infant, who by this time was sheltered in a house in David's hometown (Matthew 2:11). Why? Perhaps they believed that the Hebrew God would never discharge sacred truth to a company of Persian Magi, stargazers, announcing the "Jewish" Messiah's birth to these types. In their pride and spiritual arrogance, I believe they reasoned that only the highest levels of rabbinical scholarship would receive revelation of the Messiah's arrival.

This same misconception occurs today when mature Christians who have "been in the church longer than anyone else" believe they have solo-truth and are God's special chosen. They cannot accept the fact that Christ has other sheep who are not with their flock (John 10:16). In reality, though, it is the common, simple, praying man or woman who is often marked by the Lord to hear his voice in their secret place of prayer. Never judge the truth of the message by the appearance of the messenger. John the Baptist would have placed last in the "best dressed preach-er" contest, and he hardly would have been approved by the disciplinary board at the Temple in Jerusalem, yet his voice shook the entire nation.

Christians must not allow themselves to fall into the above scenarios of unbelief.

FIVE WRONG REACTIONS FROM SKEPTICS

The skeptics of prophecy have their own challenges. Their first and foremost is to falsely believe that God no longer speaks today, and thus any warning is a man-made fantasy, void of integrity. The second mistake of skeptics is when making an attempt to judge warnings by a lack of evidence present when nothing visible is happening and not to focus on the possibility that the future holds the fulfillment. A third mistake is to totally ignore the warnings, as though by ignoring them the voices will be silenced and the warnings will vaporize into a bad memory. Israel did this twice: years before the Babylonians and Romans crossed their borders bringing destruction, the religious critics were unable to see what was coming, tagging the prophets' words as over-zealous negative warnings, not matching the prosperity the nation was at that moment enjoying. The fourth mistake being made by many Americans is to believe they will be exempt from coming danger. They are supposedly "good people," and God would never bring anything bad on someone who is good. This was actually the blind-faith attitude among many citizens before Jerusalem's destruction—that God loved Jerusalem so much that he would protect it and never destroy it, since "God needed Jerusalem." Some in America feel the same way about America, which can be a false impression. The fifth mistake is not to plan in advance for any trouble brewing on the horizon. I see many Christians who are passive with the attitude, "I am not concerned about anything bad happening—it will all pan out." This is blind perception and lazy passivity.

IS PREPARATION A LACK OF FAITH?

Some Christians wrongfully believe it demonstrates a lack of faith to prepare for a future calamity or disaster. Months ago, a discussion ensued about the dangerous earthquake zones in the United States. It is public knowledge that the San Andreas fault line, located in California that stretches for 800 miles, is rumbling beneath the surface, and Californians have long been warned that the "big one" (a massive earthquake) is coming. It could hammer California at any moment. There is also the New Madrid Seismic Zone, a major seismic fault line that runs for 150 miles through the southern and Midwestern United States. The New Madrid system was responsible for a major earthquake that struck the Midwest in 1811-12, shaking windows as far as Washington, D.C. This seismic system stretches through Illinois, Missouri, Western Tennessee, and Arkansas and lies three to fifteen miles under the earth's surface. Seismologists have projected that should the San Andreas system produce the highly anticipated big quake, 35 million homes would be damaged or destroyed along with tens of thousands of businesses. Should the New Madrid trigger, university researchers from Illinois and Virginia Tech projected that if the quake reached a 7.2 magnitude, there could be 86,000 casualties and 3,500 fatalities, along with 715,000 buildings damaged or destroyed and economic losses estimated at $300 *billion* dollars.[9] When these two systems were discussed in my presence recently, a person in the room said, "I'm not concerned about any of that. The Lord will take care of everything." In my mind I questioned, *Is that type of thinking really "faith" or simple denial or perhaps just passivity?* I went to the Bible for my answer.

THE WARNINGS OF DESTRUCTION

The premier example of a nation being warned of future destruction is Christ's predicting to his generation the future destruction of Jerusalem and desolation of the sacred Temple. The content of this discourse is recorded in the latter section of Matthew 23 and the early portion of the Olivet discourse in Matthew 24. In Luke 21, Luke the physician presents more details of this upcoming event. When compiling the information listed by these eyewitness, we gain a clear imagery of Christ's attitude toward national destruction and his concern that his own disciples not only be aware, but also be *prepared* with an evacuation plan in place, prior to the actual destruction episode unfolding.

First, Christ gave a warning as to *what* would occur. When speaking of the Jewish Temple in Jerusalem, he predicted that "Not one stone would be left upon another that shall not be thrown down" (Matthew 24:2). Luke adds that the city would be "laid to the ground" (Luke 19:44), meaning leveled. Christ also predicted the major sign they would recognize, knowing that the destruction was eminent: "When you see Jerusalem compassed (surrounded) by armies, know that the desolation thereof is near" (Luke 21:21). Amazingly, Christ gave a more specific time frame as to *when* this terrible catastrophe would unfold when he said, "Verily I say unto you, all of these things (desolations) shall come upon this generation" (Matthew 23:36). Based upon the time frame of Israel's wandering in the wilderness recorded in the Torah and Psalm 95:10, God was grieved forty years with the generation that came out of Egypt and with the original Hebrews who departed in Exodus 12. All died in the wilderness except Moses (who died before entering the land) and two older men, Joshua and Caleb (Numbers 14:24). Christ cautioned that the coming desolation could occur within one generation, and his disciples would have understood from Scripture that it would be an average of forty years. If Christ spoke this prediction around 32 A.D., then within forty years all of his warnings concerning the toppling of the Temple stones and the destruction of Jerusalem would be fulfilled within a forty-year span.

Finally, Christ gave any disciple heeding the warnings and seeing the Roman armies marching toward Jerusalem a plan of escape. Luke wrote: "And when you see Jerusalem compassed with armies, know that the desolation thereof is nigh. Then let them, which are in the midst of it depart out; and let not them that are in the countries enter there into" (Luke 21:20-21). In the Olivet discourse Christ further instructed: "Let them which be in Judea flee to the mountains: let him which is in the house top not come down, to take anything out of his house; neither let them which is in the field return back to take his clothes" (Matthew 24:16-17).

The fourth century fathers Eusebuis and Epiphanius of Salamis both wrote that before the destruction of Jerusalem in 70 A.D., the Christians in Jerusalem were "given an oracle" (verbal prophetic warning) to escape out of the city, and many did so, fleeing across the Jordan River to a Decapolis city in Jordan named Pella. Epiphanius makes mention that the disciples of the apostles had encountered great spiritual results ministering in Pella prior to the destruction and were reporting the amazing signs and miracles occurring to leaders in Jerusalem, when an angel of the Lord warned the believers to make an exodus from Jerusalem to Pella, which the Christians in Jerusalem did. Thus, Christ's warning of *what* was coming gave a sign to indicate *when* it would occur, emphasizing the need to escape from the danger zone. It was not a "lack of faith" that the Christians left before the destruction, but rather a strategy to save their lives, as Josephus wrote that the Romans surrounded the city, stopping any food from entering. The people in the city, starving, were attempting to eat the leather on their shoes, and one woman went as far as to boil her child. Jews were busting down doors looking for even a morsel of food, and when the Romans broke through the walls, thousands of Jews were slain, including women and children, by the Roman Tenth Legion. Remaining in the city, attempting to defend it, was an automatic death sentence, and any survivor was either slain or taken as a prisoner to Rome.[10]

A TIME TO STAY AND A TIME TO GET OUT

This escape before destruction was not a "lack of faith" that moved the disciples away from the danger zone; it was God protecting a remnant from being slain in the city. In the early church in Acts, wealthy believers were selling their property and distributing the income to the needy in Jerusalem, not only to assist their poor brothers and sisters in Christ, but knowing the city would be decimated, why hold on to land and houses, when within a generation, nothing would remain (Acts 2:25; 4:34; 36-37)? It is also interesting that when Christ delivered the man of Gadera from 2,000 demons, the cured man spread his testimony throughout the Decapolis, ten cities among the Gentiles, later drawing massive crowds from these cities to hear Christ minister in Galilee. This led to countless miracles, healings, and conversions. Christ's miracles and the spread of the Christian faith many years later granted favor among the citizens and to the disciples fleeing Jerusalem, opening the doors to Pella, one of the ten cities of the Decapolis situated south of the Sea of Galilee.

There will be times when believers will receive advanced warning of danger that lurks in a particular place or a possible selective judgment that is coming. Humans can create their own crisis, such as when people start fires that burn woods and homes. These are not "judgments" but manmade disasters. If a major flood comes, and a levy is not properly built, a levy can break, causing watery destruction. The water is not God smiting evil but man's lack of integrity and work ethic. In the past, cars have crashed because brakes failed (a mechanic's failure) and planes have crashed because of pilot error (e.g., thinking they had enough fuel when they didn't). When it comes to floods, fire, hurricanes, tornados, and earthquakes, devastation comes to the righteous and unrighteous as it "rains on the just and unjust" (Matthew 5:45). However, when scientists and other informed experts warn of coming destruction, it is not "if" but "when," and it is not a lack of faith to be prepared with what is needed to ride out the storm or provide for your family in a crisis.

IS A WARNING FEARMONGERING?

Some would suggest that it is "fearmongering" to instruct people to be prepared for a natural disaster. Prophetic ministers are often accused of creating fear of the future when posting prophetic warnings of danger or possibly a judgment cycle coming to a region or the nation or world. However, Paul wrote that Noah "warned of God of things not seen being moved by fear, prepared an ark for the saving of his house" (Hebrews 11:7). This was not a "spirit of fear," which God does not give (2 Timothy 1:7), as the wrong type of fear creates "torment" (1 John 4:18). However, there is a "fear of the Lord" that brings wisdom (Psalm 111:10). When a person responds to God's warnings they are wise and understand the fear of the Lord. The best verse to sum up being prepared in advance is in Proverbs: "Go to the ant, thou sluggard; consider her ways, and be wise: which having no guide, overseer, or ruler, provides her meat in the summer, and gathers her food in the harvest" (Proverbs 6:6-8). And "A prudent man foresees the evil, and hides himself: but the simple pass on, and are punished" (Proverbs 22:3).

An example of a prudent man is Joseph. After interpreting Pharaoh's dream, Joseph set out a plan to store grain for seven years. Perhaps people mocked him, just as they did when Noah prepared the ark. However, when famine came, Egypt and the surrounding nations were spared massive casualties from starvation. Each person must hear from the Lord on his or her own and not be moved by speculation (which often occurs) but by revelation, which is the unveiling of something concealed. The Lord said he would do nothing unless he reveals his secret to his servant the prophets (Amos 3:7). Listen to praying people and not self-appointed, self-anointed prophetic "watch dogs." Most of all, fear God and not your circumstance.

Mockers and unbelievers are almost impossible to move toward faith as they are blind in the light and weak in wisdom.

THINGS I HAVE LEARNED FROM
WISE MEN AND HISTORY

Being a student of ancient and biblical history, I have learned several important truths that can apply to the historical cycle America is revolving in. The first is, when a nation with biblical knowledge refuses to honor God as their creator and walk in iniquity without repentance, God will eventually give up on rebellious people, turning them over to their own evil desires, or as Paul wrote, a reprobate mind (see Romans 1). The second observation is that there is a fear factor many people encounter, such as a fear of rejection, that motivates them toward a desire of being accepted by their peers. This desire overpowers their moral and spiritual convictions, leading them to spiritual or moral compromise. Peter called Lot a "righteous man" (2 Peter 2:8), and yet when the Sodomites attempted to break down his door to gain access to two strangers hiding in his house, Lot did not call the Sodomites "wicked" or "perverse" men. He called them "brethren," which is actually a term of endearment (Genesis 19:7), then compromised by offering his two virgin daughters to these wicked men. Believers can cross a dangerous line and place approval upon the un-anointed and unsanctified by speaking blessings to unrighteous individuals. Christ spoke of peace speakers and dust shakers, teaching that if a home was worthy, speak peace over it, but if they rejected the gospel, shake the dust from your shoes and get out (see Mark 5:13-15). Only true believers are worthy to receive Christ's peace.

Fear of man must never replace our fear of God, and receiving God's support is far greater than any benefit from men. In Israel's history, when the king separated

God from government, eventually some form of bondage or captivity followed. This includes at times economic difficulties caused by long droughts (forty-two months up to seven years) and wars. Once a nation completely rejects God, the Lord allows "hell" to be released by removing the restraint he has set against evil men. When the hedge is removed, then the adversaries of a nation can gain access to the borders, the cities, and the heart of the country. Finally, if the righteous rule the people, the land can rejoice as righteous judgment replaces injustice. However, when the ungodly are in power there is always an unfair balance, as the ungodly will appoint and surround themselves with people who act and think as they do, bringing an unfair balance and corruption of values. In America, the "left" are only tolerant of you if you accept their moral and social views. Such individuals pass laws they themselves refuse to follow.

One political candidate running for office announced "I will protect you from the rich 1 percent," yet the majority of this person's money for their political campaign came from the businesses or personal investments of that tabooed rich 1 percent, including one six million dollar donation to a super PAC from a billionaire! If you or I missed paying our yearly federal taxes, we can be targeted for an audit, penalized with interest, or, worst-case scenario, be sent to jail. Yet some federal government officials who owe back tax money often enjoy leniency, as IRS investigators turn the other cheek to prevent a scandal. These political hypocrites protest the rich, yet they scream about global warming and air pollution while flying their private jets to fundraisers with millionaires. They speak at anti-gun conventions while concealing their bodyguard's firearms, and they use the poor as pawns in voting cycles—all the while dangling a carrot on a stick to draw them to a voting booth, and after winning, put away the carrot until four more years.

FIVE URGENT MESSAGES FOR AMERICANS

There are five prophetic directives and messages that American citizens, especially the body of Christ, need to hear and comprehend right now. The first is this: America as the leading Gentile empire and world's great superpower is moving in the fast lane of going spiritually blind, and blind on purpose. We are choosing darkness rather than light. This blindness is evident with their willingness to accept what God rejects and reject what God accepts. Paul warned Timothy that in the last days, some churches will accept and approve abominable practices while at the same time reject the power of God (2 Timothy 3:5; 1 Timothy 4:1-3). Paul prayed for the "eyes of understanding to be opened," indicating that the darkness or blinders on the mind must be removed (Ephesians 1:18).

The second message for America is that the "tares" are now maturing alongside the "wheat." My wife Pam and I have discussed a "political" observation that is somewhat of a mystery to both her and me. How can Spirit-filled, Bible-toting, churchgoing, choir-singing Christians, who claim to believe God's Word is true, vote for any man or woman who unwaveringly promotes legalized abortion and the selling of infant body parts and who has no difficulty rejecting traditional marriage? My wife's answer was, "These individuals are the tares that are mingling in with the wheat Christ alluded to, that grows together until the time of the end, and only Christ and his angels can separate them at the end of the age." She is correct.

According to the parable, both will grow together, in the same field, until the final harvest (Matthew 13). How were these tares planted in the church? In the parable, the tares were sown by an enemy while the owners of the field "slept" (Matthew 13:35). I have observed in over four decades of ministry that many Christians have become passive, unguarded, and lukewarm, which has allowed the seeds of mixed doctrine and carnality to creep in and take root in their hearts. Lukewarm people breed spiritual laziness, and a slothful person is inept to guard anything.

When a true Christian promotes or aligns with any person whose values are unbiblical, unethical, or immoral, and those same values are publicly accepted by a Christian, then other believers who truly know the Word of God can see the value change of the alleged Christian and have the responsibility to question if what is hidden in his or her heart is actually matching what they confess with their mouths. We are reminded that we are "not to judge others," but it requires little discernment to "inspect the fruit" and see that it is rotten on the tree! Even Christ said, "By their fruits you shall know them" (Matthew 7:20). Just as a fountain cannot produce bitter and sweet water at the same time, a legitimate follower of Christ cannot have the mind of this world and the mind of Christ. Paul prayed that the mind of Christ (his way of thinking and believing) would dwell in every believer (Philippians 2:5).

The third message and observation concerns the mingling of *sheep* and *goats* in the church. Sheep and goats are both part of a flock. Yet goats are often difficult to deal with compared to sheep. In some traditional churches, a controlling set of goats often runs off the young lambs (youth) in the church, paralyzing the future of that local assembly. I once drove through Bradley County, where I live, on the backroads enjoying a summer ride in my convertible and passing through numerous small rural communities. I was told that in Bradley County there were about 380 different churches—more churches than almost any county in America. As I drove, within five miles, I passed three small but beautiful rural churches sitting empty, for sale. Years ago they were full, but sadly, as the congregations grew older, they never replaced those who passed away with new people, and the youth left long ago.

There is a reason sheep and goats are kept separated and among themselves. Christ spoke of a judgment in which the sheep would go to the right and enter the kingdom as the goats were led to the left and be separated in the kingdom. The "sheep people" feed the poor, clothe the naked, visit the sick, and care for the prisoner. The goats refuse to help others in any manner, are controlling and self-centered, and are at the judgment separated eternally from Christ (see Matthew 25:32-41). A believer must choose which side he or she will take and understand the consequences of that choice.

The fourth observation is simple, but important. When a spiritually ignorant or unwise individual rules in America or is positioned in the federal decision-making level, often the more conservative Christians will be heard moaning and wallowing in their complaints, later calling on intercessors to intercede for a better person to replace corrupt or bad leaders. Perhaps one of the reasons the Lord seems to do little or nothing about the wicked in charge of a nation, including corrupt leaders, is because his own people voted them in. Why should the Lord intervene in what you allow or permit?

A prime example is when the people chose Saul as their first king. God warned Israel of numerous dilemmas their future king would create for them, and yet they overrode the warning. They chose Saul from Benjamin as king, who was outwardly impressive, "goodly" (KJV), meaning handsome, and taller than all other men (1 Samuel 9:2). Israel did get what they wanted, but over time they did not like what they got! Many military men fighting in Israel's army with Saul left the backslidden king, who was weak when challenging enemies, and began following David. The best choice is to make the right choice when given a choice and choose those who best align with the principals penned in the sacred texts.

The fifth message is that America will fall in one day, and may I add, in my opinion, the rapture of the church will be the ultimate judgment against America. It will be when multitudes are suddenly missing, including state and government leaders who know the passwords to computers in offices, banks, transportation systems, military communications, satellites, and all forms of telecommunications. It will leave a nation paralyzed and in chaos, as our entire nation and world operates using electrical gadgets requiring passwords, PINs, eye scanners, and fingerprints. In Noah's day millions were sent to a watery grave when violent waters smashed the world, manifesting a judgment unseen before, after 1,556 years from Adam. In Lot's time, the sun rose across the eastern mountains as it had hundreds of thousands of mornings, but on this morning, the orange glow of the warm sun was concealed by rolling pillows of black smoke rising like a furnace into the atmosphere, choking the light on a day allowing no one, except four souls, to escape the fiery judgment on the twin cities of Sodom and Gomorrah. Just as only eight people were in the ark and only four originally escaped the path of destruction in Sodom, the living people in the judgment sectors neglected to discern the warnings and were caught off guard, not knowing the day until the water and fire blanketed their cities (Matthew 24:38-42). In one hour, everything changed.

The unexpected can transform a nation in just one hour. September 11th is one day out of 365.25 days in a solar year that is forever marked as an anniversary of tragedy. It will never be known as anything else. Passengers walking the gangways to four large planes never realized their plane would never land at its destination and that eternity was hovering just miles away. Thousands of World Trade Center workers pressed the same number on the elevator, as they did five days each week, riding it to the upper floors to work stations, lifting a cup of fresh coffee to their lips, laying their briefcase on a desk. It was just another workday. New York's twin economic towers would before noon collapse into twisted metal as rolling gray funnel clouds spun and rolled down streets. In one hour America changed. Historians admit that a democracy does not last forever. Just as Greece and Rome faded into the sunset of history, each replaced by another stronger than they, America is on this same collision course in the future.

WHEN TIME IS NO LONGER PROLONGED

We are fast approaching a time in which the unknown will become known, and prophetic insight that has been projected through years of proclamation will no longer be prolonged; it will be activated to fulfillment. Picture two trains 2,000 miles apart—both on one train track carrying dangerous chemicals and moving toward a head-on collision in a large city. Few people pay attention when the distance between the two objects is 2,000 miles apart from their crash point. As time passes, however, the distance shortens, reducing the time of impact. When the trains are twenty-five miles from the city, concern turns to panic.

Two thousand years ago, in the New Testament era, when many prophecies related to the time of the end were given to the church, time passed from one generation to another with no long seasons of fulfillment of any specific biblical predictions. In reality, from 70 A.D. to the late 1800s there were practically no end-time prophecies linked with Scripture being fulfilled. At times, however, an event would occur that would stir the minds of Bible lovers, reminding them, as per the analogy, of the two trains still on the track and moving full speed toward their colliding destination. We know from Scripture that this collision is the great tribulation. Paul noted how time would be crunched when he wrote: "For he will finish the work, and cut it short in righteousness: because a short work will the Lord make upon the earth" (Romans 9:28).

When Jesus spoke his Olivet discourse, he listed numerous signs of the end and said that when all of these things began to come to pass, people should look up for their redemption was drawing near (Luke 21:28). Throughout history, wars, famine, and earthquakes have materialized. However, Christ alluded to the "end" being when all of the signs happened at once, or when "all of these things begin." From my observation, we are the "all these things" generation.

THE AMERICAN MIRAGE

Jeremiah stood before the king, the priests, and elders only to be reprimanded, rebuked, and eventually rejected for his negative warnings that destruction was coming to Jerusalem. The holy city's inhabitants were living in a mirage of false thinking. The challenge was that prosperity blinded the people into convincing themselves that God's favor was resting upon them, despite their iniquities. No matter how much they sinned, the temple money was overflowing in the priest's coffers, the trade with surrounding nations continued, ample food supplies were available, and no outward sign could be interpreted that God was preparing a national judgment. However, this false security was all a mirage, or smoking mirrors, that deluded their perception. They were hallucinating on their own self-righteousness. They lived in a spiritual optical illusion, executing the temple rituals with the idea they alone provided a way of escaping any future dilemma, when in reality, their hearts were wicked, and their city was marked for a Babylonian invasion. Only one prophet, Jeremiah, was not drinking the wine of contentment and eating the fruit of deception.

Americans, just as ancient Israel, tend to overstate our significance and underestimate our dangers. Several years before David Wilkerson, pastor of Times Square Church, was killed in a tragic automobile accident, he received a visitation from the Lord in which he saw over 1,000 fires burning in New York. He felt this was because government assistance, such as welfare checks and food stamps, had either been cut off or were not available to those living in the inner city. One of his last warnings was when he said that one of the pre-judgment signs that God is displeased with a nation and will send judgment is when God allows extreme prosperity to come for a season, deceiving the nation into believing they are all right in God's sight. In the days of Noah before the flood, the days of Lot before the fires of Sodom, prior to Israel's exodus in Egypt, and before the Babylonian and Roman invasion, the people were eating, drinking, marrying, planting, building, and in general enjoying prosperity and success. Prosperity without purpose, though, can turn to covetousness, and Jesus said we cannot love "mammon" and God (Matthew 6:24). *Mammon* is a Syriac word (*mamona*) that denotes a god of riches, and apparently the Jews understood this word to mean wealth or money. Scholars deduct from this word the Hebrew word *'aman*, meaning to trust or to confide in because men tend to place their trust in riches and money.[11]

Do not judge the spiritual approval of God upon our nation just because the stock market is breaking records, natural disasters are infrequent, the restaurants are filled with food, and diners are profiting from consumers. These luxuries can become an American mirage that lulls a dull generation into complacency, prior to heaven visiting the nation and angels bringing back reports to God and prior to the judgment as seen in Lot's day (see Genesis 18-19). They were buying, selling, eating, drinking, marrying, and having a fine time, until the moment came.

One year after 9/11, the thought came to me that on 9/11 we became patriotic, circling the flag and singing "God Bless America," but the nation never repented. Repentance involves two main features: 1) to regret your actions and 2) to turn from sin. In America, we tend to give mercy to iniquity by glossing over the evil in the name of "loving people." If America is to be saved, America must repent of shedding innocent blood, worshipping idols, immorality, and mocking the traditional marriage covenant. This is a huge assignment, and when the pulpits are silent, the people will do what is right in their own eyes as did ancient Israel. Creating their own righteousness led them into the hands of their enemies and into captivity. Hopefully this is not the destiny of America.

5.

AMERICA—THE NEW ROMAN EMPIRE

The rise and fall of Imperial Rome is truly a foreshadowing of the American Empire. For many years I have written articles and books explaining America's unusual parallels between the Imperial Roman Empire and ancient Israel. I noted that, from a political view, America's history, architecture, and organized government is a democracy, with features comparable to the Greek and Roman forms of democracy. Israel was not a democracy but a *theo*cracy, with God as the center. It became a monarchy with the appointment of kings and eventually became occupied land under Roman dominion. The Imperial Roman Empire collapsed from within, and Israel was punished at times from within and other times from without, eventually experiencing two major exiles.

For centuries, scholars, ministers, and students of Bible prophecy have attempted to locate the United States concealed in the sixty-six books of the Bible, especially in Daniel or Revelation. These attempts have led to several prominent theories.

The first points to the four beasts in Daniel's vision in Daniel 7: the lion, followed by the bear, followed by the rise of the leopard, and a non-descriptive beast with ten horns. The traditional interpretation is as follows: the lion is Babylon, the bear is Media-Persia, the leopard is Greece, and the fourth beast is the Roman Empire, as prophetically these empires ruled in consecutive order, and Daniel does, in chapter 8, present the order of coming empires that confirms the above-mentioned flow of empires. An optional, more recent, interpretation is that the lion is a symbol of England and Britain (the British lion), the bear represents Russia (or the Russian bear), the leopard Germany (the Third Reich), and the fourth beast, the United States. While there is a point to make that modern nations can be represented with the same animal symbolism found in Daniel's vision, and at times prophetic Scriptures can have a dual application, the primary interpretation as found within the book of Daniel is the interpretation that these four beasts are the empires from Babylon to Rome. This interpretation is also confirmed by numerous early fathers.

A second, and more widespread, belief is that America is Mystery Babylon, alluded to in Revelation 17 and 18. There are various and interesting points defending this proposition. However, it would require several chapters in a book to break down verse by verse and word by word, explaining that this Babylon is more of a religious system that exercises authority over the kings of the earth. The traditional understanding is that the "Mystery Babylon" John saw was the Roman Empire, veiled cryptically by John to prevent him from being labeled a rebel against Rome. Had John stated that Mystery Babylon was Rome, the Roman leaders would have destroyed the Apocalypse Scroll, considering it a threat to the Roman Empire. The "religious" Babylon, which was a "mystery" in John's day, did not emerge until hundreds of years after John's death through the rituals and system of the Roman Church. Just as there are parallels with America connected with Rome and Israel, yet we are not Rome or Israel, there can also be parallels between the economic Babylon in Revelation 18, although we are not literally that particular prophetic Babylon.

If America's patterns, cycles, or history that is repetitive with previous empires is to be discovered, it will be in two places: Rome and Israel. The demise of these two nations will unlock the manner in which the United States could experience its own downfall.

FIRST REPUBLIC OF ROME

Classical Greece was established as a "democracy," giving its citizens the power to appoint their leaders. Rome was set up as a republic, a system with a constitution written to safeguard the rights of its citizens, both the majority and the minority. In a democracy, the rule is set by the majority—i.e., the "majority rules" through voting. In Greece, the city-states assembled to debate, and the decisions were reached by a majority vote. The assembly in Athens was known as the *ekklesia*, the same Greek word used in the New Testament translated as "church" (Matthew 16:18), and found seventy-seven times in seventy-six New Testament verses. In Athens, Greece, when the ekklesia gathered in the public square, the majority could change the leadership in the government in one day, with the majority vote—half plus one. In America, we have a representative democracy where the people elect representatives to represent their views for passing or rejecting laws. Eventually, America set up a plurality of powers, splitting the federal government into three branches—legislative, executive, and judiciary—to hopefully prevent a despot or a tyrant from seizing power from the people. The founders understood the possible "excesses and abuse" of a democracy in a majority's hands; thus, they set America as a "republic."

A republic could control a tyrannical majority both in government and with the people. A republic is built upon a constitution, which limits government's power and is "changeable" and can be amended by "we the people." For example, after the death of Franklin Roosevelt, who was elected president for four terms, Congress amended the Constitution that a president could only serve two terms, or eight years. To change this law would require the vote of two-thirds of the states and approval of both the House and the Senate. Basically, the difference between a democracy and a republic is this: a democracy is ruled by the "omnipotent" majority, and the minority has no protections over the majority. A republic centers on a representative democracy with a written constitution of basic rights protecting the minority from being unrepresented by the majority.[12]

One reason that the founders chose an electoral college when voting for the president is that if a president were elected only with the popular vote, then the large cities would always control who the president would be. With an electoral college, each state is individually represented and can participate in the process, knowing that one state may be the tipping point to who wins or loses (example, Florida in the 2000 election that George W. Bush won).

Rome was both a democracy and a republic. For example, if you were a Roman citizen, you could not be punished unless a legal trial was conducted, and you were proven guilty as charged. This is America's "innocent until proven guilty" law. Paul, a Roman citizen, was once beaten without a legal trial, and when his abusers discovered he was a citizen of Rome, they feared and requested Paul to leave quietly and not expose to the Roman leaders what they had done (Acts 16:36-40). Called Imperial Rome, the Roman Empire eventually collapsed, and the reasons have been discussed intently throughout history.

America and Rome's Three Classes

Rome basically had three classes of people, much like America. The United States is basically made up of the rich, the middle-class, and the poor. Rome was a very class-conscience society. In early Rome there were *patricians*, a wealthy elite in political power, and *plebeians*, which was the majority of Roman citizens. The upper class was divided between the senatorial class, or those in politics whose backgrounds were from wealthy, noble families. Senators had to prove they owned property valued at least 1,000,000 sesterces (a Roman coin equal to one quarter of a denarius) and did not own slaves. They were not allowed to mix personal business or trade or sign public contracts. The equestrian class was the economically wealthy, and members were required to prove their amount of wealth (property worth at least 400,000 sesterces) to be officially considered a part of the group.

The third class were the "lower classes," including the *commons*, who were all other Roman citizens; the *Latins*, who were free-born residents of Italy; *foreigners*, including the free-born men living in all other territories controlled by Rome; and the *freed people*, men and women who were once slaves but had bought their freedom or been manumitted by their masters and slaves. They were born in slavery and sold through war or piracy.

By the third century Roman law had divided the people into two main groups: the *honestiores*, or "more honorable people," and the *humilores*, the "more insignificant people." By the third century it was not the wealthy who suffered and were often penalized by Roman laws, but the commoners.[13]

Oddly, what happened to Rome after being a leading world empire is stunning. First, Rome centered its power upon its military might and ability to control provinces by placing its own leaders in positions. Since the 1990s through the early twenty-first century, America has used its military might to enter countries, removing dictators and attempting to "make peace." This was Rome's strategy through "Pax Romana," or keeping peace in Roman provinces and on borders. America has also been secretly and directly involved in nations, such as Afghanistan, Pakistan, Egypt, and other locations, overseeing the election of Arab and Islamic nations' presidents and leaders, attempting to ensure they are "pro-Western" in their ideology. America has and continues to use its military to "keep the peace" in troubled regions of the world, just as Imperial Rome did.

Rome built ships, constructed roads, built bridges, and interconnected their empire with much of the civilized world, which was a great plan. However, as years passed, the roads, bridges, and ships needed serious repairs, requiring income to be raised through heavy taxation. The tax revenue of Rome eventually became so high on farmers that many left Italy, moving to other countries as they could no longer afford the high cost of living. It has been noted that America's roads and bridges are in need of repair, and it requires billions in tax dollars to perform this task.

Rome began with good intentions of assisting their citizens who may have been out of work or needed food. Thus, a welfare-type of system emerged called "doles." Eventually, high taxes and joblessness caused many Roman citizens to depend upon the government doles for bread and income, to the point that many quit low-paying jobs, instead choosing to "live off the government." Today, America has the highest numbers of welfare recipients, food-stamp receivers, and people who receive government assistance than at any other time in her history.

Rome, with all of its wealth, enlightenment, and government regulations, fell from internal corruption, national debt, and rising taxes that the people were unable to pay. Italy was eventually overrun by invading Germanic tribes from the east who poured across the borders, taking over the vast rich farmland that for hundreds of years belonged to the Roman people. Rome's economic boom became stagnant, wages dropped, unemployment increased, manufacturing slowed, trade declined, and eventually, a dark age emerged in the western half of the empire. Rome experienced an invasion of Germanic tribes and began building defense walls across central Germany and England, as well as fortifications along the Danube, to protect the civilized people from the barbarians. These tribes would eventually seize Italy, and Imperial Rome would become history.

A WALL AROUND AMERICA'S BORDERS

Just as Rome saw what they termed the "barbarians"

coming, America has been warned for years of a barbarian-like Islamic radical movement growing in the world that is targeting the West, especially the United States. For years, America's liberal and anti-Israel leaders have publicly blasted Israel for building a concrete wall around the West Bank areas. However, this wall has proven to prevent terrorists from entering Israel, and the public bus bombings have practically ceased. America's intelligence community, men or women who will "tell the truth," are warning that thousands of terrorists have mingled with multitudes arriving illegally into America with large groups crossing our southern border. There has been a call for a large wall, which has oddly been rejected by the very politicians who have been informed behind the doors through intelligence updates that terrorists are sneaking in America and hiding in "safe houses" in towns and cities.

So much has been written about the Roman-America Empire parallels that it could fill books. However, my main concern is how Imperial Rome was tolerant of all gods and religions, except for Christianity. Christians were different from the pagans, who worshipped idols. The pagans were willing to worship the Roman emperor, when the Christians were not. The pagans never opposed calling the emperor "god," when the Christians taught there was no God but one God, and his son was Jesus Christ. Pagans saw all days of the week as work days; however, the Jews and Christians desired one day of rest set aside, and included in that day was worship of their God. By Christians giving offering to the church and not to pagan temples, the income in large Roman cities was impacted. Even in Jerusalem, there was a temple tax and Roman taxes that the Jews hated. Christians, however, gave their offering and gave no account to Rome for what was received or distributed as these were "freewill offerings," to be distributed as needed for ministry, travel, food, or assisting the needy. For Rome, religious tolerance was more about income and money than the love of the people or the support of one religion. The Christians acted in ways that were contrary to the government, leading to their persecution, arrest, and eventually thousands of deaths under Nero.

Many liberals in America have proposed to tax the churches—their land, the minister's parsonage, etc.—and remove all 501(c)(3) benefits through the IRS to ministries across America. If this occurred, thousands of churches would be forced to pay taxes, which they cannot afford, and church doors would close from coast to coast. This is the very reason the anti-Christ liberals desire this change. America's political and government patterns are parallel to Imperial Rome. And remember, Rome fell from within. Will this eventually be the end of the American Empire—an internal death by corruption, greed, and lack of morality? Time will tell.

6.

PATRIARCHS AND PROPHETS
WHO FORESAW THE FUTURE

In the Bible, some of the most unique prophecies pointing to future events are obscurely concealed in the statements, dreams, and visions of early patriarchs who are considered by scholars founders of the faith and can be considered "patriarchic prophets." While being mentioned by name in numerous biblical narratives, most of these men never wrote a book in the Bible, yet when struck by moments of divine inspiration, the scales on their natural eyes were temporarily removed. They were allowed to foresee future events, most of which would occur hundreds or thousands of years past their lifetime. Such future visionaries include Adam, Noah, Abraham, Jacob, and even Job, who spoke of a redeemer in the last days (Job 19:25).

The patriarchs were the men from the early Old Testament era, beginning with Abraham, the father of the faith, to King David, Israel's second king, who captured the stronghold of Zion. These godly men established individual and national covenants with the Almighty, forming and solidifying a covenant nation for the Hebrew people and uniting under twelve tribes called Israel. God revealed clear instruction (laws, statutes, and judgments) to his chosen people through the venue of spoken words, visions, and dreams. Abraham, Isaac, Jacob, Moses, and David were all recipients of these revelations regarding past history, present truths, future events, and prophetic scenes about what was to happen in the "last days."

ADAM AS THE FIRST PROPHET

Before detailing some of the amazing prophecies of the pre-law patriarchs, let us look at the "prophets" who were part of the first ten generations—beginning with Adam, God's first man, to Noah, the tenth generation from Adam. While many scholars mark Enoch, the seventh descendent from Adam, as the first prophet in biblical history and Scripture, it was actually Adam who, according to the Jewish historian Josephus, received the first prophetic warning of future judgments that would impact the world. It was a word that many believe was revealed directly by God to Adam and his sons at some point after Adam's fall. Flavius Josephus, the noted Jewish historian, wrote about the sons of Seth, Adam's third son, in the biblical record, and Adam's astonishing prediction of two global judgments:

> "They (sons of Seth) were also inventors of that peculiar sort of wisdom which is concerned with the heavenly bodies and their order. And that their inventions might not be lost before they were sufficiently known, upon Adam's prediction that the

world was at one time to be destroyed one
time by the force of fire and at the other
time by the quantity of water, they made
two pillars; one of brick and the other of
stone; they inscribed their discoveries on
them both, that in case the pillar of brick
should be destroyed by the flood, the pillar
of stone might remain, and exhibit those
discoveries to mankind" (Josephus; *Antiquities of the Jews; Book I*).

This prediction was known among devout Jews in the
Roman time, indicating it was a widespread belief. In a
Latin text from a document called *The Life of Adam and
Eve* (49:3-50:2), which was comprised from the Jewish
book *The Apocalypse of Moses* (first century A.D.), the same
prediction is given, but attributed to Michael the Archangel who transmitted the message to Seth though Eve. He
predicted: "On account of your transgressions, our Lord
will bring upon your race the anger of judgment, first by
water, the second time by fire; by these two will the Lord
judge the human race."[14] The message then instructs Seth
to make tablets of stone and clay to record these warnings. The idea was when the watery flood came, the clay
tablets could be ruined, but hopefully the stone will remain. And if the fire comes, the stone will be broken, but
the baked clay will remain.

In Scripture, not much history is written of Adam
after his expulsion from Eden (see Genesis 3 and 4), as
Moses began penning his ten generational pre-flood genealogies, starting in Genesis 5:1-32. This prediction would
make this prophecy, accredited to Adam, the first future
prophecy given to a mortal, after Adam's expulsion from

the Garden of Eden.

ENOCH AND THE SECOND COMING

Among the names recorded identifying the first ten righteous men, one noted prophet is Enoch, whom Moses wrote walked with God for 365 years and "was not for God took him" (Genesis 5:24). To understand this phrase, the New Testament refers to Enoch this way: "By faith Enoch was translated that he should not see death; and was not for God translated him: for he had this testimony that he pleased God" (Hebrews 11:5). Thus, the seventh man from Adam on the 365th year of his life disappeared from the planet, being caught up to heaven to be with God. The Jewish tradition is that Enoch was born at the season known later in history as Pentecost and was translated on the same calendar day Pentecost. The book of Jasher, considered sacred Jewish literature (mentioned in the Bible twice—Joshua 10:13; 2 Samuel 1:8), indicates that Enoch, just as Elijah, was actually transported to heaven in a chariot of fire, although the biblical account said he was "not for God took him" (Genesis 5:24), and "Enoch was translated that he should not see death" (Hebrews 1:5).

The book of Jude presents an interesting commentary on Enoch, which clearly indicated that he was the first man seeing the return and rule of the promised Messiah (Genesis 3:15) and that "saints" would accompany the Messiah's arrival to earth. In Jude 14-15 we read, "Now Enoch, the seventh from Adam, prophesied about these men also, saying, 'Behold, the Lord comes with ten thousands of His saints, to execute judgment on all, to convict all who are ungodly among them of all their ungodly deeds which they have committed in an ungodly way, and of all the harsh things which ungodly sinners have spoken against Him'" (NKJV).

What is fascinating about this prediction is the time it was given, prior to Enoch's translation, which was (when adding up the chronological years) 988 years from Adam, or less than 1,000 years after the fall of Adam and Eve and fifty-eight years after Adam's death. Enoch's second-coming prediction is an estimated 3,012 years prior to Christ's birth in Bethlehem, meaning that Enoch saw by divine revelation the return of the Lord before the Christ was ever manifest the first time on earth! This makes Enoch's prediction the first biblically noted prophecy predicting the return of the Lord. Notice the "saints" return with the Lord to "execute judgment," a revelation that was not fully explained until hundreds of years later by the Hebrew prophet Zechariah (chapter 14) and several thousand years later in the Apocalypse (see Revelation 19:11-16). Enoch is believed by many scholars to be one of the future two witnesses alluded to in Revelation 11.

NOAH'S PROPHECIES CONCERNING HIS SONS

All believers who have studied Scripture are aware of the Torah's narrative of the great global floodwaters washing over the planet in the days of Noah, in which Noah and seven others secured protection in a large wooden craft called an ark (see Genesis 6 and 7). If I were to ask a congregation, "Was Noah a prophet, or did he speak prophecies concerning the future?" I suggest most would say, "No, he built an ark." However, after the flood, before his three sons—Shem, Ham, and Japheth—scattered in three different directions to repopulate an empty world, an important prediction was spoken by Noah. Due to a strange episode of his becoming drunk, Noah placed a curse upon Canaan, the youngest son of Ham, stating he would be a "servant" to the descendants of Shem (see Genesis 9:25-26). Since Shem was blessed to be the superior leader among Noah's three sons, the descendants of Shem would dominate over the descendants of Ham and Japheth.

In the Genesis genealogy, one of Shem's great grandsons was Eber. It is believed that the "Hebrew" people who were descendants from Abraham through Isaac derived their name from Eber. As for the name, "Hebrew," others note that Abraham departed the land of Ur, requiring him to "pass over" the river Euphrates on his journey to the promised land. The word "Hebrew" is *abbar*, referring to *passing over*. In Genesis 14:13, Abraham is called "the Hebrew," or *ha-Ibiry* in the Hebrew language, referring to "pass over" or "come from beyond."

Clearly, the Hebrews from Abraham's loins came from Shem's lineage, and Noah predicted Canaan was to be a "servant" to Shem's descendants. Biblically, Canaan eventually settled in the land today known as Israel. Canaan was the father of numerous sons whose descendants evolved into various tribes, controlling sections of the promised land as noted in the days of Abraham and Lot. The name of the promised land in the days of Abraham was "Canaan," named after Ham's youngest son, Canaan (see Genesis 12:5; 13:12; 16:3; 17:8; 23:2). Eight tribal groups from Canaan's genealogy are named in the Torah as "the Jebusite, Amorite, Girgasite, Hivite, Arkite, and Sinite; the Avadite, Zemarite and the Hamathite" (Genesis 10:16-18). When Israel departed from Egypt to repossess the promised land, many of the above tribes were controlling important cities and hill country and were propagators of idolatry. God commanded Israel's men to uproot these tribal groups because their idols would become a "snare" to Israel's monotheistic faith in the future (Deuteronomy 7:16). Noah predicted that Canaan would not lead, but Shem would rule over him, which is historically what transpired after Israel repossessed the promised land, eventually overpowering and defeating these tribes. Canaan's descendants, the Jebusites, were in control of Jebus, which was Jerusalem, and remained in control of the city, as the early Israelites never conquered the Jebusites. However, this tribe was eventually overtaken and expelled in the time of David (see 1 Chronicles 14:4-6). Thus, Noah's prediction of Shem's dominion over Canaan came to pass.

Adam, Enoch, and Noah are three of the first ten generations inspired by the Holy Spirit to speak words revealing the future. It should be noted that a person speaking or writing a future prophecy that comes to pass may not always be a "prophet" by biblical definition. After all, the Holy Spirit can show any discerning, Spirit-filled believer "things to come" (John 16:13). However, in the Scriptures, individuals who received inspired dreams, spiritual visions, or personal angelic visitations connected with the future were often considered prophets from the Hebraic concept of thinking. Here's how Moses identified prophets: "And he said, 'Hear now my words: If there be a prophet among you, I the Lord will make myself known unto him in a vision, and I will speak unto him in a dream'" (Numbers 12:6).

While most students of Scripture view these early men whose names are found in Genesis as godly men assisting in the formation of the nation of Israel or anointed for specific purposes, various Scriptures identify several of these key leaders as "prophets." For example, in Genesis 20, in a warning dream, God demanded King Abimelech to restore Sarah to Abraham, or God would slay the king. In the warning dream shown to Abimelech, God stated that Abraham was a "prophet" (Genesis 20:7).

ABRAHAM THE PROPHET

Numerous future events, some related to Christ, were made known to Abraham. The Lord revealed to this covenant man the future of his two sons, Ishmael and Isaac (Genesis 16:11-16; 17:1-19), how his descendants would be afflicted in a foreign land (Egypt) for 400 years (Genesis 15:13), and how nations would emerge from his future descendants and all nations of the world would be blessed as a result of his obedience (Genesis 22:18). In Genesis 22 Abraham also saw by divine insight man's redemption to occur on Mount Moriah. This "vision" appeared to Abraham about the time he was offering Isaac on a stone altar. After the ram replaced Isaac, Abraham called the place "Jehovah Jirah," indicating that God would provide the final sacrifice on the same mountain where Abraham had built his altar. Moses commented on Abraham's experience writing, "In the mountain of the LORD it shall be seen" (Genesis 22:14), referring to a future "lamb" that would become a redemptive sacrifice (note Genesis 22:8). Christ told followers that "Abraham rejoiced to see my day and saw it" (John 8:56). From a Torah perspective, the only time Abraham could have "seen Christ" as the lamb was when Abraham spoke of God providing a "lamb" during the offering of Isaac on the mount (Genesis 22:8). On that day, as Abraham approached the mountains of

Moriah, we read, "Abraham saw the place afar off" (Genesis 22:4). In Hebrew, the phrase "afar off" is *rachoq* and can allude to both seeing a place *in the distance* but also *perceiving something about the future* in space and in the time to come. Abraham was on the mountain of sacrifice, the same hill where two temples would be erected, becoming the center of all sacred and spiritual activity for his future tribal clans. On this mount, the Lord instructed Israel to build a temple as a gathering place for festivals and a mountain of sacrifice and blood. The prophet Abraham saw more than a rugged mountain; he peered into the future and saw the final lamb that God would provide on his holy mountain, that lamb bringing the redemption covenant (John 1:29).

ISAAC'S PROPHETIC INSIGHT

The Bible does not record the Lord speaking in a dream or vision to Abraham's son, Isaac. However, in Genesis 27 at age 160, Isaac believed he was near death and was nearly physically blind. During a strange twist of events, his intention to bless his oldest son, Esau, was interrupted by his younger son, Jacob, who deceived him into believing he was Esau. Isaac, by divine inspiration, spoke prophetic words over Jacob's future. The prophecy spoken over Jacob was so compelling that when Esau entered the room, he realized his brother Jacob had deceptively intercepted his blessing, which was reserved for the oldest son. At the time of Isaac's prophetic word, Jacob was unmarried with no children. Jacob's name would later be changed to Israel (Genesis 32:28).

In the personal prophetic blessing to Jacob, Isaac disclosed to his son that he would prosper in the land with numerous agricultural blessings. Other nations would serve Jacob, and he would be the lord (leader) over his brothers. A word that was first spoken from God to Abraham is here repeated by Isaac when he said to Jacob, "cursed be everyone that curses you and blessed be everyone that blesses you" (Genesis 27:26-29). Later, Esau came into the tent begging his father Isaac for a personal blessing. Esau too received a prophetic word revealing his future when Isaac predicted that Jacob would rule over Esau's descendants (Genesis 27:37). It is also interesting to note that Isaac foresaw that the sons of Esau would "live by the sword," meaning Esau's descendants would be a warlike tribal group. This prediction is evident throughout the Old Testament as the sons of Esau, the Edomites, were warlike in nature and persisted in battles for many generations. Isaac, however, also peered into his son's future, foretelling how Esau would one day "break the yoke" of Isaac's posterity off his neck (Genesis 27:39-40). Today, the land of the Edomites is the modern country of Jordan. This nation has become a strong, independent society that Israel has no dominion or military control over. Israel actually enjoys peace and trade treaties with Jordanian neighbors. Thus, Isaac, for a brief moment, looked beyond his day into the future destinies of his sons. Although Jacob left home for twenty years, when he, his two wives, and children return to the promised land, Esau and he actually bonded again, and both agreed to go their ways in peace (see Genesis 32).

JACOB EXPERIENCED ANGELIC VISITATIONS

Abraham's grandson, Jacob, experienced a marvelous dream of angels ascending and descending on a heavenly ladder, whose top originated in heaven and whose base rested firmly on the earth. We know Jacob was near a place called Luz (Genesis 28:19) when this dream occurred. Many Jewish rabbis, including former Rabbi Yehuda Getz from Jerusalem, teach that this dream occurred while Jacob was sleeping on the Mount of Olives, and the massive ladder was set on Mount Moriah where Abraham had placed Jacob's father, Isaac, on an altar. When Jacob awoke from this supernatural dream, he promised God that if the Lord would bring him back from Syria, to this land, he would present God with the tithe (the tenth). Jacob spoke a prophetic declaration over the place of this visitation, saying, "How dreadful is this place! This is none other than the house of God, and this is the gate of heaven" (Genesis 28:17). The *gate of heaven* was the top of the ladder, and the house of God was set at the base of the ladder. After setting a stone pillar to mark the site, Jacob continued to predict, "And this stone, which I have set for a pillar, shall be God's house: and all that thou shalt give me I will surely give thee the tenth" (Genesis 28:22).

According to sacred Jewish writings such as the book of Jasher, the base of Jacob's ladder was set on the mountain of Moriah, the very place of Abraham's altar and the location of two future temples where all sacrifices, including the Israelite's "tithe," would be presented to God by Abraham and Jacob's descendants. This ladder dream distinguished Mount Moriah as the future site of the house of God (Temple). Jacob knew that Mount Moriah was the mountain where his grandfather Abraham encountered God's first king-priest named Melchizedek and where his father Isaac was presented to God and a ram replaced him on the altar (Genesis 22:1-4). The sacred hill was also the first place where tithe is mentioned, as Abraham presented the tithe to Melchizedek (see Genesis

14). Thus, Jacob stepped into the role of a visionary with prophetic inspiration as he perceived the place where the house of God—the Temple—would be erected, enabling his future sons' tribes to present their tithes and offerings.

In a second angelic visitation, Jacob wrestled an angel, who before departing at sunrise, performed two acts that forever changed Jacob. The first was when he touched Jacob's thigh, which created a lifelong limp that would slow Jacob down and alter his walk, causing him at the conclusion of his life to lean on his wooden staff for physical support (Genesis 32; Hebrews 12:21). The second transformation was that the angel changed Jacob's name from Jacob to Israel, a name in Hebrew meaning "who prevails with God." Jacob's sons were called the "sons of Jacob" or "Jacob's sons" before going to and while living in Egypt (Genesis 49:2). However, before experiencing deliverance, marching as an army out of Egyptian bondage, they are called the "children of Israel," as God wanted them to understand they were going to prevail over the Egyptians as "Israel" and not "sons of Jacob" (Exodus 1:1).

THE PROPHECIES OF JACOB

Moses records in Genesis 49 that when Jacob was dying, he gathered his sons to his side, speaking a final word related to their future. Jacob began his discourse with these words: "Gather together, that I may tell you what shall befall you in the last days" (Genesis 49:1). Notice that the timing for the prophetic fulfillment is the "last days." Jacob proceeded to proclaim either blessings or disfavor on his sons, including their future living conditions, opportunities for certain blessings, and special activities they would engage in as metaphors that unlocked God's mysterious plans for his sons, once they possessed the promised land. If we should break down verses, individual words, and phrases, it would require an entire chapter in this book to expound on each son's personal prophetic forecast and how and when each prediction was fulfilled. However, I wish to focus on the prophetic word spoken over Jacob's fourth son, Judah. Jacob detailed Judah's future in the following passages:

> "Judah, thou art he whom thy brethren shall praise: thy hand shall be in the neck of thine enemies; thy father's children shall bow down before thee. Judah is a lion's whelp: from the prey, my son, thou art gone up: he stooped down, he couched as a lion, and as an old lion; who shall rouse him up? The scepter shall not depart from Judah, nor a lawgiver from between his feet, until Shiloh come; and unto him shall the gathering of the people be" (Genesis 49:8-10).

The Hebrew name "Judah" originates from the Hebrew root *yadah*, meaning "to hold out" or "extend the hand," especially in reference to worship. Thus, Judah's name is associated with praise and worship to God. The prediction of Judah's hand being on the neck of his enemies was evident during Israel's conquest of Canaan. It was Caleb, the eighty-five-year-old strongman in Judah's tribe, who defied three giants in Hebron, running these towering threats off a mountain he had claimed forty years prior, an example of fulfilling the prediction of Judah's dominion over his enemies (Joshua 14:11; 15:1; Judges

1:1-2). King David defeated the Philistines and their giant champion, Goliath, just as Christ, a thousand years later, stripped the satanic hosts robbing death of its sting and depopulating hell's future inhabitants. Both David and Christ were born in Bethlehem, a city in the heart of the tribe of Judah. David, when defeating his enemies, quoted Jacob's prediction in Psalm 18:40: "Thou hast given me the neck of mine enemies, that I might destroy them that hate me."

Jacob spoke of Judah being a "lion's whelp." Judah began as a young lion (a whelp) and eventually matured into a powerful "old lion." Because of this prophetic imagery, a lion became the emblem of the tribe of Judah on their military standard. When David conquered Jebus, making it Jerusalem, one of the new names David gave Jerusalem was "Ariel," meaning the "lion of God" (1 Chronicles 14:17; Isaiah 29:1). Christ, after he defeated death, hell, and the grave, is called "the lion of the tribe of Judah" (Revelation 5:5), as he alone prevailed against his spiritual enemies: Satan, death, and hell. Jerusalem was a part of Judah's land grant, and in the 1950s the coat of arms for Jerusalem included a lion.

Jacob's prediction continues, when explaining that the scepter (the authoritative rule through kings and monarchs) of Judah will remain in political and spiritual control of the region of Judea until just prior to the arrival of Shiloh (Christ). This occurred when Judea was placed under the control of a Roman deputy, and taxes were issued by the governor of Syria (Luke 2:2).

The most interesting part of Jacob's prophetic vision for Judah is that "Shiloh" would come. In the eighth century B.C., when the ten northern tribes separated from Judah and Benjamin, the tribe of Judah remained faithful to

God and to the Temple for many generations. Jacob predicted that Judah's "scepter," a metaphor for ruling and political control, would "not depart" until Shiloh comes. Shiloh was the location where the tabernacle of Moses was pitched for hundreds of years (Judges 18:31). However, the geographical area of Shiloh is not in the tribal area of Judah, but Ephraim—thus, this name, Jacob, alluded to in the prophecy was not Shiloh the city. Shiloh is also a metaphorical name used to identify the future king-ruler of Israel from the tribe of Judah. It is widely held that Christ was born between 2 to 1 B.C. based on new evidence. At this time, the Jews in Judah had lost governmental authority of Judah as the Romans began controlling all political appointments in the territory; thus, the scepter departed from Judah. Jacob's words for Judah built the foundation upon which Messianic expectations were seeded in the hearts of the following generation. Mary and Joseph were both from the house of David, with family roots in the city of Bethlehem.

DAVID'S STUNNING PROPHETIC INSIGHTS

Peter, during his sermon on Pentecost, quoted from a psalm that he applied to Christ's resurrection (Acts 2:27). Peter publicly stated what all devout Jews in his day believed: that David was a "prophet" (Acts 2:29-30). David's penned numerous prophecies are now identified as Messianic predictions, including his detailed foreknowledge of the Messiah ruling in Israel, his violent sufferings, and his kingly rule from Jerusalem. Beside these, many psalms paint a vivid picture of the future destiny of Israel, the Jews, and Jerusalem.

Some of the most detailed Old Testament predictions

revealing Israel's suffering Messiah are written in Psalms; the most astonishing is Psalm 22. We will highlight several verses that have a direct fulfillment as recorded by New Testament eyewitnesses of Christ's sufferings at his crucifixion.

Psalm 22 begins, "My God, my God, why hast thou forsaken me?" This phrase was one of seven sayings Christ spoke from the cross. Matthew and Mark both narrate the crucifixion scene when Christ said, "My God, my God, why hast thou forsaken me?" (Matthew 27:47; Mark 15:34). In Psalm 22:6 it was written, "But I am a worm, and no man; a reproach of men, and despised of the people." Isaiah confirmed this prediction when he wrote, "He is despised and rejected of man; a man of sorrows and acquainted with grief" (Isaiah 53:2-3). Christ was mocked (Psalm 22:7), and in the Psalms we read this sentence: "He trusted on the LORD that he would deliver him: let him deliver him, seeing he delighted in him" (Psalm 22:8). This exact phrase was repeated by religious mockers at Christ's crucifixion when they taunted Christ, saying, "He saved others; himself he cannot save . . . He trusted in God; let him deliver him now; if he will have him for he said I am the Son of God" (Matthew 27:42-43).

The psalmist then depicted the physical plight of Israel's suffering Messiah when he wrote, "I am poured out like water, and all my bones are out of joint: my heart is like wax; it is melted in the midst of my bowels. My strength is dried up like a potsherd; and my tongue cleaves to my jaws; and thou hast brought me into the dust of death" (Psalm 22:14-15).

Jesus said, "I thirst" (John 19:28), which agrees with David's words, "My tongue cleaves to my jaws." Perhaps the most dramatic and revealing phrase is the latter verse found in Psalm 22:16: "they pierced my hands and my feet." This was clearly a picture revealing *how* the Messiah would be brutally slain—by crucifixion. This verse was written 500 years before crucifixion was practiced as a capital punishment. The first recorded instance was in 519 B.C. when Darius I, King of Persia, crucified 3,000 political enemies.[15] It was the Romans who perfected the execution process of a crucifixion, using it for 500 years until this wooden execution system was abolished by Constantine in the fourth century. The Roman soldiers chose not to rip apart Christ's seamless garment, choosing instead to cast lots and give the winner the garment as a prize (John 19:24). This unknowingly fulfilled Psalm 22:18: "They part my garments among them, and cast lots for my vesture."

The death and resurrection of Christ initiated and sealed a new covenant ratified by Christ's shed blood. This universally available eternal blessing is to be preached in all nations in a message called the gospel (Matthew 24:14). Christ's great commission to preach the gospel to the world aligns with Psalm 22:27, which says, "All the ends of the world shall remember and turn unto the LORD: and all the kindred of the nations shall worship before thee." There are five Scriptures in Psalm 22 quoted in the New Testament that are fulfilled through Christ, which makes this chapter one of the most significant prophecies of Christ, not only in Psalms, but in the Old Testament (with exception of Isaiah 53).

It was also written in Psalm 16:10: "For thou wilt not leave my soul in hell; neither wilt thou suffer thine holy one to see corruption." This verse would make little sense without understanding that the subject here is a resurrection from the dead, *prior to the physical body deteriorating.* In

Christ's day the Jews buried the dead before sunset, on the same day of their death, and since they normally did not embalm the corpse, the natural decaying process caused the body to begin deteriorating by the beginning of the fourth day (note Lazarus in the tomb in John 11:39).

Christ's body was wrapped in 100 pounds of linens and spices and raised at the end of three days (John 19:39-42). In Acts 2, on the festival of Pentecost, Peter was proclaiming the resurrection of Christ, quoting this psalm and relating its fulfillment to Christ's supernatural resurrection. Peter addressed his Jewish audience by saying, "For David speaking concerning him, I foresaw the Lord always before my face, for he is on my right hand, that I should not be moved . . . Because thou wilt not leave his soul in hell, neither wilt thou suffer thine holy one to see corruption" (Acts 2:25-27).

David also knew that the Lord would one day rule on earth as King and alludes to the Lord being "King" thirty-seven times in Psalms. Another fascinating verse in Psalms explaining the timing of the Lord's return as linked to the prosperity of Jerusalem is in Psalm 102:16. We read: "When the Lord shall build up Zion, he shall appear in his glory."

Psalm 102:16 mentions "Zion" and not "Jerusalem." Zion is the mountain in David's time where the city of David was constructed—a steep slope on the southern hills of Jerusalem. Zion was the hill, and Jerusalem was the name of the city that expanded to the north on the plateau of Mount Moriah where Solomon constructed Israel's first sacred temple to God. Zion is linked with the monarchy of King David while Jerusalem is identified by future generations as the single chosen location of God's House, the Temple. This was the city where God "put his name" (Deuteronomy 12:21) and called the "apple of his eye" (Zechariah 2:8).

With the reestablishment of Israel as a nation in 1948, Jerusalem was divided by "Arab East Jerusalem" and the Jewish sector in the western half of the city. Large concrete walls divided not only the city but also determined which side lay claim to a particular territory, as Jordan controlled the east side and Israel the western half. After the June 1967 Six Day War, Israel annexed East Jerusalem, the concrete barriers were shattered, and barbed wire was ripped from its stronghold. In 1967 Jerusalem's population was 263,307, and today Jerusalem is Israel's largest city with a population of over 800,000. This makes up 10 percent of Israel's population, with the second largest city being Tel Aviv.[16]

Jerusalem in Jewish hands, the expansion of the city in seven different directions, and the fact that all nations travel to Jerusalem to visit the Holy places and pray is a fulfillment of "Zion" being "built up." David notes the Messiah's priestly ministry when saying, "Thou art a priest forever after the order of Melchizedek" (Psalm 110:4). Psalm 110:4 is confirmed as a fulfillment through Christ in Hebrews 7:17: "Thou art a priest forever after the order of Melchizedek." David noted the strong authority of Israel's future king Messiah when he predicted he will "break them with a rod of iron" (Psalm 2:9). This verse is quoted in Revelation 2:27 to the church at Thyatira: "He shall rule them with a rod of iron." These are just a small sampling of many predictions from the mouth and the pen of David, a true prophet and king.

DAVID SAW CHRIST'S RETURN

One of the most detailed insights into the return of Christ

was written a thousand years before Christ's birth, and now over 3,000 years have passed: "Our God shall come, and shall not keep silence: a fire shall devour before him, and it shall be very tempestuous round about him. He shall call to the heavens from above, and to the earth, that he may judge his people. Gather my saints together unto me; those that have made a covenant with me by sacrifice. And the heavens shall declare his righteousness: for God is judge himself" (Psalm 50:3-6). David's fine points in these passages agree with the words of the apostle Paul.

In these verses, the Lord is returning from heaven to the earth with the saints. The Lord is coming from heaven, as Paul wrote that the Lord shall be "revealed from heaven" (2 Thessalonians 1:8). The psalmist noted that a fire was round about him, which agreed with Paul when he said the Lord would come "in flaming fire" (2 Thessalonians 1:8). As the Lord "calls to the heavens above," this would be his call to the saints in heaven, making up the "armies of heaven" that will be descending from heaven to the earth "riding upon white horses" (Revelation 19). The Lord is returning to "judge" his people. Paul said that when Christ returns he will take "vengeance on those that know not God and obey not the gospel" (2 Thessalonians 1:8).

The scene suddenly shifts in the verses to the Lord instructing to "gather my saints together unto me." This may indeed be an early reference to the gathering together of the living and the dead at the rapture of the church and resurrection of the dead in Christ. Writing of this event, Paul said, "we shall be caught up together . . . to meet the Lord in the air" (1 Thessalonians 4:17). Those being gathered together are those who have made a covenant with God. Only those in covenant will be gathering together with Christ.

Here we again see that David was a unique prophet who foresaw the Messiah's first appearing and sufferings but also viewed the future and saw the Lord return to earth with the saints. Not only did David see this gathering together, but Job also gives us insight into the righteous resurrection.

JOB'S RESURRECTION REVELATION

Believers never think of the book of Job as concealing any prophetic insight. The book is viewed as a struggle with understanding the pain and suffering of the righteous and teaches how steadfast faith endures and outlasts trials. However, several powerful prophetic proclamations are found in Job's discussions with his friends. It is believed that the events in Job occurred in the time of Moses, and Moses may be the author of the book. Job 19:25-27 reads: "For I know that my redeemer liveth, and that he shall stand at the latter day upon the earth: And though after my skin worms destroy this body, yet in my flesh shall I see God: Whom I shall see for myself, and mine eyes shall behold, and not another; though my reins be consumed within me."

Here, the Lord is called Job's "redeemer," which can now be understood as the redemptive covenant provided by the Lord that promises a resurrection of the righteous. Job said the Lord his redeemer would "stand at the latter day upon the earth." This prediction is repeated in numerous verses, including Isaiah 59:20: "And the Redeemer shall come to Zion." Zechariah said the Lord's "feet will stand that day upon the Mount of Olives" (Zechariah 14:4), which matches Job's prediction that "he shall stand . . . on the earth." In John's apocalyptic vision he saw Christ return to earth "with the armies of heaven" (Revelation 19:11-16). Job gave the time of the Lord's standing on earth as, "In the latter days," a phrase referring to the final days of man's governmental rule on earth that end when the "stone kingdom" will come crashing down on the nations, consuming them like chaff on the threshing floor and conceding their kingdoms to Christ, who will set up his thousand-year kingdom in Jerusalem (see Daniel 2:30-35; Revelation 20:4).

Job's "skin worms" refers to the death process: a physical body returns to dust, and the bones return to earth. Job understood that when the Lord returns, he will raise the righteous dead, giving them a new immortal body in which they will "see" the Lord (1 Corinthians 15:51-54). In Job 14:10-14, there is another section of verses that uncover more prophetic insight.

> "But man dieth, and wasteth away: yea, man giveth up the ghost, and where is he? As the waters fail from the sea, and the flood decayeth and drieth up: So man lieth down, and riseth not: till the heavens be no more, they shall not awake, nor be raised out of their sleep. O that thou would hide me in the grave, that thou would keep me secret, until thy wrath be past, that thou would appoint me a set time, and remember me. If a man die, shall he live again? all the days of my appointed time will I wait, till my change come."

From verse ten through verse fourteen, there are several significant words and phrases, indicating that Job received a divine revelation of man's death process and the future resurrection. Job began by revealing that when a man dies he "gives up the ghost." This phrase of giving up the ghost alludes to the human spirit departing from the physical body at death, as confirmed with Abraham (Genesis 25:8), Ishmael (Genesis 25:17), Isaac (Genesis 35:29), Jacob (Genesis 49:33), and Christ (Mark 15:37), all of whom "gave up the ghost," meaning their spirits exited their bodies at death. The book of Job records this separation at death as a fact, and hundreds of years later the apostle Paul reaffirmed that when we are "absent from the body we are present with the Lord" (2 Corinthians 10:11).

The second remarkable truth established is in verse twelve, revealing that the "heavens would be no more!" This prediction is well documented by the prophet Isaiah, who spoke of a "new heaven and new earth" (see Isaiah 66:17, 22), and in Revelation 21:1 where John also observed a "new heaven and a new earth." There will be a group of the unrighteous dead that will be raised at the end of Christ's thousand-year reign to stand before God at the Great White Throne judgment. Most scholars believe while this judgment is materializing in the heavenly Temple, at the same time, the earth will be renovated by fire, and a new earth will form (2 Peter 2:12-13; Revelation 20:11). The souls of these individuals will remain in *sheol* (under the earth) until the time of this judgment and the passing of the heavens, just as Job indicated here!

Job asked if a man will "live again," pointing to a resurrection. He answered his own question, saying that he would wait (in the grave) until his "change" would come. The Hebrew word here for "change" means to "alter something." Paul wrote that when Christ returns "we shall be changed" (1 Corinthians 15:51-52). Thus, Job received a dynamic revelation of the resurrection when the decayed bodies in the grave will be raised and "changed" at the resurrection of the righteous. We should note that while it appeared to Job's "friends" that the Lord had forsaken Job, notice the number of times throughout the book that Job speaks by a divine revelation. Thus, his circumstances may have appeared to isolate him from God, but Job's divine inspiration from the Lord was not hindered by his circumstances.

THE GREATEST PROPHETIC INSIGHT IS FROM MOSES

There can be no doubt that Moses stands alone as the premier prophet of God in the Old Testament, if not one of the most noted of all times. Moses knew God intimately, saw God on Mount Sinai, and experienced the visible manifestation of God's glory on numerous occasions. The fifth book of the Torah, Deuteronomy, concludes with this statement: "And there arose not a prophet in Israel like Moses, whom the Lord knew face to face" (Deuteronomy 34:10). It was Moses whom God inspired to write the first five books of Scripture, called the Torah, concealing within the narratives numerous types and shadows of God's concealed plan for mankind's redemption and voicing future warnings for Israel, once they settled in the holy land.

Four of the major stories that clearly reveal God's plan of redemption are, first, Genesis 22, where Abraham offered his only son Isaac on Mount Moriah, laying him on wood as a sacrifice. This ancient account paints the imagery of God the Father sending his only son Jesus Christ to Mount Moriah to be offered on a wooden cross, the ultimate sacrifice for mankind's redemption.

The second, and perhaps most recognized, imagery of future redemption is the patterns of Passover, narrated in Exodus 12, where the blood of a lamb was placed on the left, right, and top posts of the door, restraining the death angel from entering to slay the firstborn. These three blood markings were a preview of three crosses to be erected on Golgotha, where the blood of Christ, God's lamb, was being poured out for man's atonement. As the people *ate all of the lamb* that night, a mass healing occurred, and on the morning of the exodus not a feeble person was found in any tribe (Psalm 105:37). This event was a double cure—redemption from death and healing of their bodies. Christ was beaten with stripes and nailed to the cross—one was for our physical, emotional, and spiritual healing and the other for our redemption from sin and death.

Turning to Numbers 19, Moses set rules for a rather strange sacrifice: the burning of a red heifer. This female sacrifice was offered "without the camp." The priest would cast cedar wood, hyssop, and scarlet thread into the sacrificial fire, afterwards collecting the cow's ashes and mixing them with pure water for ritual purification. Moving ahead 1,500 years, the sacrifice of the heifer is parallel to Christ's crucifixion, as he was crucified "without the gate" (Hebrews 13:12). A scarlet robe was placed over his shoulders, he was nailed to a wooden cross, and hyssop was used dipped in vinegar to help deaden the pain, which Christ refused (see Matthew 27). Christ's sacrificial blood purifies the sinner from all uncleanness.

Numbers 21 illustrates another fascinating type and shadow of the Messiah. Israel's rebellion had led to an act of God's judgment, sending vipers inflicting deadly venom to all they bit. God instructed Moses to build a brass pole, wrapping a brass serpent around it and hoisting it into the air, providing instant healing to those bitten. If they would look, they could live. Christ referred back to this story, comparing it to his future crucifixion. He foretold, "As Moses lifted up the serpent in the wilderness, even so must the son of man be lifted up" (John 3:14). The binding of Isaac (Genesis 22), the lamb's blood at Passover (Exodus 12), the red heifer burning (Numbers 19), and the brass snake on the pole (Numbers 21) were illustrations that later confirmed Christ was the fulfillment of these types.

THE PROPHECIES CONCERNING ISRAEL

Rabbis who have poured over the words and individual letters in the Torah have noted Moses' specific predictions involving events that would befall Israel in the "latter days." Moses accurately foretold of a day when Israel would, because of their disobedience and unrepentant sins, be removed from the land and taken into captivity in other nations for an extended season. One warning is often applied to a description of dread and anxiety during the Nazi Holocaust.

> "And among those nations you shall find no rest, nor shall the sole of your foot have a resting place; but there the LORD will give you a trembling heart, failing eyes, and anguish of soul. Your life shall hang in doubt before you; you shall fear day and night, and have no assurance of life. In the morning you shall say, 'Oh, that it were evening!' And at evening you shall

say, 'Oh, that it were morning!' because
of the fear which terrifies your heart, and
because of the sight which your eyes see"
(Deuteronomy 28:65-67).

Clearly, the entire Bible from Genesis to Revelation is
a book inspired by God and filled with verses, paragraphs,
and entire chapters of predictions, many of which have
come to pass, and over one-third remaining to be fulfilled.
As seen in this chapter, some of the most unique predictions are found concealed within the stories of the men
who are not marked by contemporary scholars as significant prophets, but they were prophetically inspired. These
holy men gave us a foreshadowing of not only events related to the redemption of mankind, but also to the events
revealing the return of Christ.

7.

BIBLICAL NUMBERS AND THE HEBREW ALPHABET REVEAL THE ELECTION CODES

In the mid-1980s, just after my first tour to the Holy Land, I began what has become a lifelong journey into the study of the Hebraic roots of Christianity. For me, this translated into an emphasis on Old Testament prophecies, the amazing Hebrew alphabet, and the Hebrew language at large. Being raised in a traditional denomination and in a pastor's home to boot, the majority of what I was exposed to early in life was the twenty-seven books of the New Testament. I seldom recall any study centering on the Old Testament prophets, and almost nothing from the Torah. In those days, the Sunday school literature was focused on the gospels and the writings of Paul. The general feeling among church members and certainly denominational officials was that we Christians were "New Covenant" people. Many believed the Old Testament had, as they said, "been done away with." We were constantly reminded that the Old Testament was "part of the law," and as New Covenant people, we were "no longer under the law." My own study and research, however, convinced me that the

Old Testament was the New Testament concealed, and the New Testament was the Old Testament revealed.

After several Bible courses from Lee College, including Old and New Testament surveys, I realized that the apostles in the New Testament consistently quoted the Torah, the Psalms, and prophets—the so-called Old Testament. The reason these early believers did so was to prove to the Jews that the Torah and Prophets testified that Jesus was the promised Messiah (see Acts 28:23). The book of Revelation alone makes direct or indirect references to the Old Testament about 550 times. Furthermore, from the viewpoint of prophecy, hundreds of Old Testament prophecies are yet to be fulfilled. For example, Ezekiel chapters 38-48 are all considered to be future and, as of now, unfulfilled events. These and other facts led me to go from being only a New Testament ministry to being one that studies and researches truths from the *whole Bible*. Not only that, but I determined to analyze the Old Testament from a Hebraic perspective primarily because the majority of the Old Testament, with the exception of a few portions in the minor prophets that were written in Aramaic, was written in the Hebrew language.

My subsequent yearly pilgrimages to the Holy Land solidified my desire for a better understanding of the Hebraic perspective of Scripture. During the early 1990s, I encountered one of Jerusalem's leading rabbis, Yehuda Getz, who, before passing in 1995, was the chief rabbi of Jerusalem's Western Wall. In this position, Getz also oversaw the ongoing excavations in the area I call the "Rabbi's Tunnel." Officially, it is known as the Western Wall Heritage Foundation. Through the influence of my friend and guide, Gideon Shor, my wife Pam was the first woman granted permission to walk behind locked doors to see a secretive excavation that was exposing ancient arched vaults. After meeting with Getz and hearing his explanations and insight concerning the Ark of the Covenant, God imparted an inspiration into my spirit. I came away wanting to understand Bible prophecy from the Hebraic point of view and investigate rabbinical wisdom on biblical subjects, including the seven festivals of God and other festivals such as Hanukkah and Purim.

I soon discovered that Hebrew words lose some of their deeper meaning once they are translated into English, or other languages for that matter. Also, I learned that Hebrew words stem from three-letter root words, and that understanding the root of a word—even the individual letters in that root—often unlocks amazing insight that will unfortunately go undiscovered in different translations.

MYSTERIES IN THE HEBREW ALPHABET

In the late 1980s I became very intrigued with the Hebrew alphabet. In the beginning of the process I learned that Hebrew is read from right to left, rather than left to right. The alphabet has twenty-two letters with no vowels. It does have a system of dots and dashes, though, called *nikkud*. They are written above, below, or inside a letter that tells the reader what vowel sound to pronounce. I also learned that one of the most interesting aspects of the Hebrew alphabet is that each letter has a symbol or picture, and consequently different concepts, connected to it. For instance, the first letter, *Alef*, is symbolized by an ox. The second letter, *Beit*, is a house. The third letter, *Gimel*, represents a camel, and so forth. The final letter is *Tav* and is symbolized by a cross.

Another interesting point is that each Hebrew letter can be expressed with a numerical value—beginning with the first letter, *Alef,* whose value is one, and ending with *Tav*, which has a value of 400. This intrigued me, and over the years, I have thoughtfully researched the link between the alphabet and its symbolic and numerical system. Here is why this should interest Christians: there are times when the numerical values linked with Hebrew letters can reveal biblical precepts as well as prophetic patterns and seasons.

The system rabbinical sources use to calculate the numerical values of individual letters, words, or phrases is called "gematria" and dates back at least as far as the Babylonian captivity, perhaps longer. In fact, the prophet Jeremiah used a derivative of this system to refer to Babylon, cryptically, as Sheshach (Jeremiah 25:26, 51:41). The word *gematria* comes from the Greek word for "geometry" and is related to the word *grammateia*, meaning "knowledge of writing." The system is used primarily to gain insight into biblical concepts by finding words with the same value. Oftentimes, these matching words are related not just in numerical value but thematically too; therefore, we discover the connection between these different words and see how the language itself bolsters truths presented to us in the Scripture.

For instance, the value of the Hebrew word for "child" is forty-four; the value of the Hebrew word for "blood" is also forty-four.

Among the rabbinical rules of hermeneutics, four levels of understanding are used to interpret the Scripture. The first is called *peshat* (the literal and simple meaning). The second is called *remez* (a hint or allusion to other Scriptures). The third is *derash* (homiletical study), and the fourth is *sod*, which is the secret, or mystical, meaning. It is this fourth level of understanding that I want to emphasize because it has great bearing on our subject matter.

Experienced rabbis who follow the four levels of interpretation do so in order to better understand spiritual concepts and mysteries. One of the methods they employ as they seek this understanding is analyzing the Hebrew alphabet and its numerical system. For the most part, this way of approaching Scripture is either unknown or labeled as taboo among most Western theologians. Most Bible schools and Christian universities view the Old Testament as history and Hebrew as archaic, emphasizing the New Testament and the Greek language instead. Yet, we need to realize that mysteries are embedded or hidden in Scripture and the Hebrew language itself. This is not an exclusively rabbinical or Old Testament point of view.

In multiple gospel accounts, Christ brought his disciples aside in order to teach them the "mysteries of the kingdom" (Matthew 13:11). In his letter to the congregation in Ephesus, Paul spoke of a mystery God had hidden from the foundation of the world that was made known to him so that he might present it to the church (Ephesians 3:3-9). Paul also spoke of the "mystery of redemption" and other prophetic mysteries throughout his epistles; in fact, he used the word *mystery* seventeen different times. Paul even referred to ministers as "stewards of the mysteries of God" (1 Corinthians 4:1).

Also, both Christ and Paul made clear that spiritual mysteries are most often concealed from the wise of this world and only revealed to the "babes," or young, in Christ who are hungry for God's wisdom. Pharaoh's wise men and soothsayers were incapable of interpreting his dream, for example. It was a young Hebrew named Joseph who was ultimately summoned from prison to give the king an answer to the mystery hidden within his dream (Genesis

41:14-16).

One example of gematria I'd like to share with you is looking at the sacred name of God, YHVH (alt. YHWH), pronounced by most as *Yahweh* or *Yahveh*. In Hebrew, reading left to right, it is spelled יהוה (*yod, hei, vav, hei*). The numeric value of the letter י *yod* is ten, the value of the letter ה *hei* is five, and the value of ו *vav* is six. When you total the value of the letters (remember there are two ה) the total is twenty-six. It has been noted that the original Temple Mount was approximately twenty-six acres. When God spoke to Moses of the place where he would bring the children of Israel, it was a place where he would "put his name" (Deuteronomy 12:5; 14:23).

Another interesting example is the phrase "the Satan," pronounced *ha'satan* and which means "the adversary." Reading left to right, it is spelled השטן (*hei, siyn, tet, nun*). The numerical value of this word is 364, and that is important for this reason: There are 365 days in a solar year—one more than the value of the word *ha'satan*. Rabbinical commentators take note of this difference and interpret it to mean that there is one day of the year when Satan has no power over your life: the Day of Atonement! Yom Kippur, or the Day of Atonement, is when God will not entertain the accusations of the adversary and forgives Israel of their sins.

WHAT ABOUT THE CRITICS?

Over forty years of ministry have taught me many things. One of the things I have learned is that people are very skeptical of what they do not understand.

In the late 1980s, a team of Israeli professors led by Eliyahu Rips released findings of their research into what would become known as "Bible Codes." Their conclusion was that the Bible, specifically the Torah, possessed a mathematical element whereby encoded messages could be uncovered by searching the Hebrew text in equidistant letter sequences (for example, skipping every seventh letter). This was not a new concept—it had been observed and written about decades before. But with the advent of computers and the development of specialized programs, greater amounts of text could be searched and at greater speeds. To the amazement of Rips and his colleagues, the words and phrases they discovered in the text were such that it went beyond being explained away as random occurrences in a voluminous text. To the contrary, statistical math proved that "someone" had deliberately embedded these "codes" into the Bible.

During one of my trips to Israel I learned of this research and, in time, presented it to churches and those who followed our ministry. While some found it as fascinating as I, there was a widespread negative reaction. Perhaps the most surprising thing about the negativity is that it sprang primarily from ministers. I heard comments like "There are no such things as Bible codes" and "The Bible means what it says and says what it means." I was constantly ridiculed with claims that I "had gone off the deep end with all that Hebrew stuff." A few went so far as to label me a heretic. In time, however, these skeptics found it difficult explaining away the mounting evidence that there was something to the research. Supporters pointed out the verse where Daniel was told that at the "time of the end, knowledge will be increased" (Daniel 12:4). Until the development of computers, observing these codes on this scale would have been almost impossible; with increased technology, though, came increased knowledge. As you might expect, most of the negative comments came from those who did little to no research on the subject. Unfortunately, ignorance of the subject did little to abate their outspokenness and criticisms.

People also criticize the notion that gematria is a valid method of understanding the Scripture, much less interpretation. Many choose to acquaint it with numerology and practices associated with the occult. It is true that there is a perverse use of numbers, values, and their supposed meaning, but I believe that the adversary targets anything that is true and pure in an attempt to pollute and discredit it. For instance, there is a study and understanding of the stars in the cosmos called astronomy, and there is a perversion of this understanding called astrology. When it comes to the validity of numbers in Scripture, I'd like to call your attention to a passage from the Apocalypse.

Revelation chapter 13 predicts the rise of a person with the nature of a wild beast who we call the Antichrist. That same chapter describes a second beast who is also known as the false prophet. John reveals that this false prophet will obtain complete control over buying and selling by using a mark—the name of the first beast or the *number* of his name. Without having any of these identifiers, a person will not be able to purchase or to sell. I firmly believe that in the passage following these revelations, John alludes to gematria when he says: "Here is wisdom. Let him that hath understanding count the number of the beast: for it is the number of a man; and his number is six hundred threescore and six" (Revelation 13:18).

In some early Greek codices, this passage is not written with the Greek words that would be translated "six hundred threescore and six," but with three Greek letters: *chi*, *xi*, and *sigma* (in antiquity, called "stigma"). As with

Hebrew, each Greek letter has a numerical equivalent. The numerical value of these letters does in fact add up to 666, although these three letters spell nothing. Couple this with the fact that the text instructs the reader to "count (or calculate) the number of the beast." In later translations, these three letters became "six hundred threescore and six." It is very likely that the same use of gematria employed by Jewish rabbis today was known to John in his day. It is also probable that some similar use of the Greek alphabet was in use at the time, and that is why John, considered a "mystic" due to his use of strange prophetic symbolism in the book of Revelation, used these three Greek letters to convey a hidden message.

For the past several years, I have carefully used this system in search of possible clues that would help me discern what God is speaking prophetically for the near future, specifically as we enter the New Year on the Hebrew calendar. I have been criticized for doing this; however, as the expression says, "the proof is in the pudding." Each year, both on the Hebrew and Gregorian calendar, I have shared with those who follow our ministry the possible meanings of these years based on the Hebrew alphabet. In other words, the numbers in the years are exchanged with the corresponding Hebrew letters; sometimes these letters form words. Sometimes, the ancient form of these letters—remember they all started as pictographs—might also paint a picture of what God is speaking prophetically for that year. Thankfully, during each year, what I have presented to the public has proven to be on target. For instance, those who heard me speak of the year 5777 and the forty-fifth president, long before the election, know that the pattern I suggested was fulfilled on election night much to my own amazement! I'll discuss that in more detail later.

While this system is intriguing and interesting to all who love the Bible, I want to issue a word of warning, especially to those who are casual students of the Bible and mere curiosity-seekers. Human nature is, when interests are piqued, to drift toward extremes. I have seen Christians become so deep into Hebrew-related teaching that they begin to ignore, even reject, foundational doctrines of the Bible. In extreme cases, some have abandoned Christ in order to follow rituals or traditions that are of little spiritual value. While understanding the unique and amazing nature of this type of research, every Christian should be fully aware of the pitfalls when one doesn't abide by the eternal laws of sound biblical doctrine, especially those present in the gospel of Christ (Romans 1:16).

NUMBERS AND THE BIBLE

The use of numbers began with creation, where we see that God numbered days from the *first* to the *seventh*. The seventh was a day of rest, the Sabbath (Genesis 1 and 2). In fact, in Hebrew, the days are known as Day 1, Day 2, etc. It was the Romans who named the days of the week after different gods in their pantheon. The first day of the week, Sunday, was so named after the sun god; Monday was named after the moon god, and so on. The Romans also did this with the months of the year: January, for instance, was named after the god Janus. Throughout the Old Testament, the months of the year—though many are given a name—are repeatedly referred to by number, whether it be the seventh month (Genesis 8:4), the ninth month (Ezra 10:9), or what have you.

From a biblical perspective, all numbers found in

Scripture have a meaning based on either the law of first mention or distinct incidents connected with those numbers. For example, the number three represents unity; persons, places, and things are grouped in threes throughout the Bible. The number four is linked with the earth; there are four points on the compass, four rivers that branched out from the one river in Eden, and four gospels that detail Christ's earthly ministry. The value five is connected with the concept of grace, six is always a number tied to mankind (man was created on the sixth day), and seven is called a number of completion and perfection. Seven is used extensively when speaking of heavenly events or narratives connected to God himself.

The number forty is related to testing. Israel wandered for forty years in the wilderness, Goliath taunted Israel for forty days, and Jesus was tempted by Satan for forty days. The number fifty is the number of years counted in order to determine the year of Jubilee, and seventy is related to the completion of judgment and exile. These are but a few examples, but hopefully you see, from a biblical perspective, that once a number in Scripture has been associated with a particular theme, that association never changes.

THE ANGEL OF NUMBERS

The book of Daniel expresses numerous examples of prophetic events revealed to the prophet in dreams or visions. The book also mentions certain angels—at some times, Gabriel, and at other times, an unnamed angel—who assign specific timeframes to the particular prophecy they announce (see Daniel 8:14, 12:7, 11-12). In chapter 8, the prophet relates a situation in which he overheard a conversation involving a "certain saint" (Daniel 8:13). In the marginal notes of some older KJV translations, this Hebrew word translated as "certain saint" is understood to be the angel Palmoni, a name meaning "the number of secrets."

In 1902, F. C. Gilbert, a Jewish man who had received Christ, wrote the book *Practical Lessons for the Church Today*. In his book, Gilbert noted that this "certain saint" was indeed Palmoni; in fact, the word *saint* is only implied, not stated definitively in Hebrew. Some rabbinical scholars believe Palmoni is an angel specifically assigned to deal with prophetic themes and numbers, especially in regard to Daniel's prophecies. The Hebrew word *palmoni* is derived from two Hebrew words (read left to right): הלפ *palah*, meaning "wonderful," and הנמ *manah*, meaning "to number" or "enumerate."

If we had only the book of Daniel to go by, we could easily see that biblical concepts associated with numbers are important in God's prophetic plan. In Scripture, God assigned a festival to a specific month and day, never altering the time frame (Leviticus 23). God ordained every seventh day as a Sabbath day of rest. He determined that every seventh year was to be a *sh'mitah* and the conclusion of every forty-nine-year period (seven times seven) was to mark the beginning of the Jubilee.

As the Bible describes the time of Noah's flood, we see that numbers and various time frames are found throughout the narrative. These examples include:

- "take by sevens" (Genesis 7:2)
- "yet seven days" (Genesis 7:4)
- "six hundred years" (Genesis 7:6)
- "forty days and nights" (Genesis 7:12)
- "fifteen cubits" (Genesis 7:20)

- "one hundred and fifty days" (Genesis 8:24)

The story also mentions the "seventeenth day" (Genesis 8:4), the "tenth month on the first day" (Genesis 8:5), "seven days" (Genesis 8:10, 12), and the "second month on the seventh and twentieth day" (Genesis 8:14)—and that is just two chapters!

After years of Bible reading, study, and research, I can attest that the various numbers in the Scripture all have meanings inserted into each respective narrative by divine inspiration. In other words, these numbers are not inserted into the story just for information; they are placed there because, at times, they reveal prophetic themes, parallels, and cycles that recur throughout history.

While analyzing numbers and their alphabetic equivalent may appear to some as uninteresting, controversial, or downright strange, I believe the insights gained can further validate the Bible as the inerrant Word of God. More than just a clever document penned by religious zealots with wild imaginations, the Bible is the expressed will of the creator—able to save, deliver, and transform mankind. And like its author, it is limitless and unfathomable, evidenced by the fact that it continues to reveal mysteries and secrets reserved for those living in the time of the end (Daniel 12:4).

THE REMEZ FACTOR

As previously stated, Jewish rabbinical studies approach biblical exegesis on four different levels. The fourth level is called סוד *sod*, which is the level where mysteries are concealed. The second level is called רמז *remez*, referring to things that are "hinted at," or alluded to, but not definitely stated. One way this method is demonstrated is found in

Psalm 34:7, which says, "The angel of the LORD encampeth round about them that fear him, and delivereth them."

Literally, the verse says that those who fear the LORD have the promise of divine protection. The *remez* found in this verse is what is not stated, yet strongly implied: those who do not fear the LORD have no such promise.

Another way of understanding this concept is by observing the law of double application, which is to say, understanding that a prophetic passage can apply to more than one situation. An example of this is found in the Gospel of Matthew, where the angel commanded Joseph to take his family to Egypt in order to escape Herod's order to kill the child. After Herod's death, Joseph is then commanded to return to his home, as Matthew recorded, "that it might be fulfilled which was spoken of the Lord by the prophet saying, 'Out of Egypt have I called my son'" (Matthew 2:15). Matthew's statement is actually a quote taken from the book of Hosea where God, speaking to the prophet, identifies Israel as his son and says: "When Israel was a child, then I loved him, and called my son out of Egypt" (Hosea 11:1).

In Hosea, the verse was referring to those Moses led from Egypt to Canaan. Fifteen centuries later, the "son of God," Jesus Christ, spent a brief season in Egypt only to be called out to return to Israel, thus fulfilling the prophecy in Hosea—even though it didn't at first seem to be a prophecy at all. This is just one of many examples in Scripture where what was written of those living in the era of the Old Testament was observed by the New Testament writers as having a parallel in the ministry of Christ. It is also a great example of how things not definitely stated are, nevertheless, inferred in the text—a *remez*.

This double-law factor can be explained this way. Man

lives in a three-dimensional world, but God exists in multiple dimensions. He dwells in light that no man can approach (1 Timothy 6:16) and transcends time itself. That means God exists in the past, present, and future and is not confined to any one dimension. Likewise, his Word transcends time and is not limited to any one dimension. Just because a verse can be interpreted one way doesn't mean that it is the only way to understand it, and just because it applies to one event in time doesn't mean it can't apply to another event in another time.

The Word of God can have, as my friend Dr. Bryan Cutshall says, "layers" of understanding: it can be literal, allegorical, and metaphorical and can present patterns, types, and shadows. While something in Scripture can express something very plainly, it can also contain a mystery that will be revealed at a later time. The account of the brass serpent on the pole (Numbers 21), for instance, recounts something that actually happened to Israel in the wilderness, but it also contains the mystery of Christ's crucifixion as he explained to Nicodemus in John 3:14, centuries after the incident.

As I've already pointed out, these "layers of understanding" include things that are hinted at in the Hebrew language, including the symbols represented by the individual letters as well as their numerical value. That being said, I want to take a look at the recent election cycle to see if there are clues that hint at prophetic themes and if the Hebrew language may give us further insight into what God was, and is, saying through the U.S. election cycles.

THE TRUMP EFFECT

It is hard to imagine that there could have ever been a more controversial and divisive presidential election than the one between Al Gore and George W. Bush in 2000. But then came 2016. In my view, the election of 2016 eclipsed the contention of 2000 by light years. The most contentious development, of course, was the unexpected election of Donald Trump. To say it was unexpected by most is a gross understatement; to millions, it was unthinkable—the equivalent of a political shock wave. Most major newspapers and nearly every media outlet had Hillary Clinton winning the election by a landslide. Going into Election Day, she enjoyed a two- to three-point lead, prompting some pundits to predict her winning with as many as 320 electoral votes. To their surprise, millions of rural Americans in "fly-over country" and the Rust Belt voted for Trump, giving him the edge even in states that seldom vote for a Republican presidential candidate.

From the time of Bill Clinton through the election of Barack Obama, the Holy Spirit has inspired me with insight, either before the election or shortly thereafter, into how biblical figures are mirrored by these high-profile political figures. To recount all of the information I've shared concerning Clinton, Bush, and Obama from start to finish would require a very voluminous book. Suffice it to say, those previous insights have proven to be 100 percent accurate. Now, however, I want to look at the possible prophetic themes and patterns connected with the election of Donald Trump.

Because of past predictions, ministry partners began asking me what I was feeling about the 2016 presidential race. Initially, my thoughts went to a 1933 prophecy, which spoke of a time when driverless cars were on American highways, and a woman rose to power as a leader—possibly president—of the United States. Hillary Clinton seemed to fit this scenario perfectly. However, when I learned that the Hebrew year, which began on October 2, 2016, would be the year 5777, I began to look at an alternative outcome. I began researching the Hebrew letters connected with this Hebrew year to see if a prophetic pattern emerged.

THE BIG "WHAT?"

On election night, November 8, 2016, one hour before my son turned on the big screens at Omega Center International (OCI), I shared a prophetic observation with the packed auditorium about who would win the election. I told them that when it was over, people would be in disbelief, saying, "What?!" I then shared how I arrived at this conclusion. It involved the system of exchanging numbers for letters in the Hebrew alphabet.

I pointed out that the president-elect would become the forty-fifth U.S. president. Since each letter of the Hebrew alphabet has a numerical value, forty-five can be written with two Hebrew letters: מ *mem* (the value being forty) and ה *hei* (the value being five). These two Hebrew letters form the Hebrew word *mah* and means "what." While all Hebrew letters have a numerical equivalent, not all Hebrew letters combined in this manner necessarily form words. In this case, it turned out that the value forty-five—corresponding to the forty-fifth U.S. president—would be linked to "what."

As I said, the secular media was convinced, without any doubt, that Hillary Clinton was destined to be the next president of the United States. It was reported that the Clinton camp was already picking a transition team, making plans to relocate to Washington, and, allegedly, referring to Clinton as "Madam President." Even before all the polls had closed, she was receiving congratulatory phone calls. All of the exit polls had her ahead in most battleground states, assuring her of a win . . . but then the bottom fell out.

When Florida was unexpectedly called for Trump, the tide changed suddenly. As the numbers came in, and more and more states were called for Trump, the secular media went into shock, and when the election was finally called for Trump, plenty of pundits were left with egg on their faces. Many saw the outcome as proof that there was still a strong remnant in America who perceived that the nation was in trouble and that Clinton had to be stopped. Their vote was saying, "We don't like where the nation is going and want it changed." But in the early morning hours of November 9th, when Trump was named the forty-fifth president of the United States, media members were shaking their heads in disbelief and asking, "How did this happen?"

I will never forget the moment, three days later, when Fox News personality Megyn Kelly uttered these words: "This election has left the American people saying, 'What?'" I sat there stunned with my mouth hanging wide open. There it was: the outcome that sent a shockwave throughout the country, confounding the political elite, secular media, Hollywood, and all those who had anointed Hillary as the next leader of the free world.

IN THE YEAR 5777

The Gregorian calendar and the Hebrew calendar differ in many ways. The Hebrew calendar is lunisolar, meaning that it is determined by both the moon and the sun. The Gregorian calendar is strictly solar. The Hebrew calendar is believed to date back to the time of Adam, whereas the Gregorian calendar goes back only to the advent of the Christian era. That is why we mark time in terms of B.C. (before Christ) or A.D. (abbreviated form of the Latin phrase *Anno Domini*, "in the year of our Lord"). Because of this difference, the Gregorian calendar says we are living in the twenty-first century; the Hebrew calendar says we are living in the fifty-seventh century.

The 2016 presidential election occurred on November 8, 2016, which, on the Hebrew calendar, was the seventh and eighth of Cheshvan, 5777 (the date changed from the seventh to the eighth at sunset). It is rare, indeed, to see three sevens appear in one year. In fact, this will not be repeated again for a thousand years (6,777). As an interesting footnote, on the Gregorian calendar, the last time three sevens appeared in this manner was in the year 1777. In that year, the Continental Army began winning battles against the British, and the Articles of Confederation were adopted by the Continental Congress as our first "constitution." You could say that this is when the tide began to turn toward American independence.

When writing the Hebrew year in Hebrew characters, 5777 becomes עשתה״ז. Reading from right to left, the last character, the ה *hei*, represents the value 5000. The thousands place is understood because there is no Hebrew character having the value of 5000 (by the way, there are no Hebrew characters that have the value zero). In fact, the year 5777 is commonly written without the *hei* עש״ז. Thus, the actual year becomes 777. The calendar year—three sevens—is written as ת *tav*, ש *shiyn* (their combined values being 700), ע *ayin* (whose value is seventy), and ז *zayin* (the value being seven). But let us also look at it this way: three individual sevens or three of the letter ז *zayin* (the Greek letter *zeta*, the seventh Greek letter).

There are several ways in which rabbis have interpreted the letter *zayin*. It is taught that the form of the letter in its ancient form represents a scepter or rod, symbolizing the authority of a king or other such ruler. It is also taught that its form represents a "sword" or a "sharp weapon." The hint, or *remez*, of this letter, as taught by rabbinical tradition, is "while pointless bloodshed is certainly not the ideal, we sometimes must fight in order to defend our lives and our way of lives."[17] Perhaps this is why the *zayin* is said to resemble the flame of a torch, alluding to a light in the midst of darkness.

It is also taught that *zayin* is actually the letter ו *vav*—the sixth letter in the Hebrew alphabet—with a large crown placed upon its head. Because six is the biblical number representing man or mankind, the *zayin* can be considered the crowning of a man, giving a man the rod or scepter of authority. Thus, *zayin* is a man of authority. Couple this with the fact that, on the Hebrew calendar, three sevens appear in the same year that many Americans were stunned when a powerful businessman was elected president over a lifetime politician; I believe this has deep meaning when looking at it from a Hebraic perspective.

THE LARGE ZAYIN IN MALACHI

In the Hebrew Tanach, there are places in the text where a Hebrew letter will be written smaller or larger than its normal size. Rabbinical commentaries advance the idea that these "scribal errors" are not errors at all but were written this way purposely. But for what purpose? Traditionally, these variations in size are viewed as markers intended to provide insight into a deeper message within that particular word or passage. Malachi 4:4 provides just such an example: "Remember ye the law of Moses my servant, which I commanded unto him in Horeb for all Israel, with the statutes and judgments" (Malachi 4:4).

In the Hebrew text, the first letter in the Hebrew word for "remember" is *zayin*, and it is written slightly smaller than normal. Seeing that the *zayin* can represent a sword, the hint here would be that remembering the law (literally, Torah) of Moses would constitute a weapon to use against all forms of spiritual adversaries in the future. The next passage, Malachi 4:5, predicts the future appearance of Elijah the prophet, sent by God to turn the hearts of his people back to him and his Word.

Elijah, in this text, is believed to be the literal Elijah— the same man who departed the earth in a heavenly chariot and will return as one of the two witnesses during the tribulation. However, because prophecies can have double meanings, we must also consider the role of the "spirit of Elijah." The Bible tells us that John the Baptist came in the spirit and power of Elijah and, because of that anointing, spoke uncompromisingly and with boldness. This is the type of spirit America needs to see in its ministers and political leaders as we approach the climax of the end of the age.

THE MESSAGE WITHIN TRUMP'S NAME

The traditional tomb of King David is located under a tourist site called the Upper Room, a place presented as the room where the Last Supper was held, although the building likely only dates to the thirteenth century. Rabbi Yosef Berger currently oversees this Jewish holy place located atop Mount Zion. It was Rabbi Berger who made this observation: the numerical value of the Hebrew phrase "Messiah for the house of David" is 424. It just so happens that this is the same value of the Hebrew spelling of Donald Trump. It must be noted that this, in no way, suggests that Donald Trump is some type of Messianic figure or savior. However, might it suggest that his election comes at a crucial time as we approach the Messianic era? Trump's stated position regarding Israel has been favorable, even as his stand against radical Islam enemies is unquestionable. If he, in fact, follows through on his positions, it would sync with the Jewish expectations of a leader expected to emerge prior to the age of the Messiah's appearing.

One rabbi has been quoted as saying, "When political developments reflect what is written in the Torah that is a clear indication that we are nearing *ge'ulah* (redemption). God is taking over directing events."[18] Against all odds, Donald Trump was elected president of the United States, which prompted numerous respected rabbis in Israel to state what many Americans refuse to acknowledge: the outcome was the will of God—plain and simple.

TRUMP SEVENTY PLUS SEVEN PLUS SEVEN

In the English translation of the Bible, the word or value "seven" is found 463 times; "seventh" is found 120 times. The biblical meaning of seven is a completion of time or a cycle, also signifying perfection. Some even refer to seven as God's sacred number. Consider the seventh day Sabbath and the seven yearly festivals, three of which fall on the seventh month called Tishri. In the book of Revelation, Jesus addressed the seven churches of Asia. There is also the seven-sealed book and the seven bowl and trumpet judgments, and finally, there are seven thunders as well as seven angels dispensing the different judgments (Revelation 1:20; 5:1; 8:6; 10:4; 15:1).

Since the 2016 election came during the first few weeks of the Hebrew year 5777, we will again look at the numerical equivalent of the Hebrew letters, focusing on the three sevens and how they may relate to the election of Donald Trump. He was born on June 14, 1946. His inauguration occurred on Friday, January 20, 2017. Trump's first full day as President was January 21, 2017. From June 14, 1946, to January 21, 2017, Trump was seventy years of age plus seven months and seven days: seven—seven—seven.

Based on what we have learned, the three sevens and their connection to Trump's age at the time of his inauguration and assumption of office hints at something. Perhaps it is a sign from heaven that we are coming to the completion of a cycle and transitioning from one prophetic cycle to another. Maybe it is to signal that, within the next few years, God will initiate the fullness or completion of the "times of the Gentiles" and the time commonly referred to as the "Church Age" (Ephesians 3:2). Only time will tell if these possibilities prove to be accurate as we move toward the next election cycle in 2020.

THE TORAH READING "CODES"

With each new Hebrew year, the Torah reading cycle both ends and begins. By that I mean that the last portions in the book of Deuteronomy are studied and then, on Simchat Torah (rejoicing in the Torah), the scroll is rolled back to the beginning, Genesis. With that, the cycle is renewed, and for every week following, synagogues around the world read the same portion of Scripture. As I have already pointed out, many times we see that significant world events have a parallel event within the Scripture being read that particular week. This phenomena brings to mind what is recorded in Ecclesiastes: "That which has been is that which shall be and that which is done is that which shall be done" (Ecclesiastes 1:9-10).

As I mentioned earlier, when Barack Obama was sworn into office in January 2009, the most recent Torah portion contained the verse that recalled the rise of a new pharaoh who had no regard for Joseph and, by extension, the Hebrew people. It was that pharaoh who concocted policies designed to place heavy burdens upon God's people. I, along with Bill Cloud, suggested that Obama would not be a friend of Israel and would impose burdens upon the people of God. After eight years, this projection proved accurate. Not only did Obama support Israel's enemies, but he also released hundreds of millions of dollars to Iran, opening the door to the development of nuclear arms by a rogue and radical Islamic government. Instead of combatting Islamic extremism and promoting liberty, he placated the Islamic world, encouraging the likes of ISIS to rise and spread terror. At the same time, he was passively aggressive toward Israel—at least until the end of his presidency. In the last weeks of his tenure, his true feelings toward the Jewish state were laid bare.

Not only that, but Obama's domestic agenda speaks for itself as well. By his words and actions it is obvious that he harbored contempt for traditional, even biblical, values in deference to a progressive, liberal anti-biblical agenda. The White House was illuminated in celebration of same-sex marriage, but not so in support of fallen law enforcement officers. It certainly seems that the Torah reading just before his inauguration proved to be an omen of his leadership and unbiblical tendencies toward God's people.

Knowing this, I was curious as to what the Torah reading would be the weeks leading up to the inauguration of Donald Trump. Would there be clues that gave insight into a prophetic pattern? Would history, once again, repeat itself? According to the set schedule for the year 5777, the Torah reading for the two weeks January 1-14, 2017, was Genesis 44:18 through Genesis 50:26.

THE UNEXPECTED SWITCH

One of the fascinating events within these chapters in Genesis is found in chapter 48. It is recorded here that Joseph brought his two sons before his father, Jacob, for a blessing. He expected that his oldest son, Manasseh, would receive the right hand of blessing, which would identify him as the chosen leader among the two. Yet, at the very last minute, Jacob switched his hands and placed his right hand of blessing on the younger son, Ephraim. This broke with long-established tradition and protocol, even to the point of provoking Joseph to protest, rebuking his father and trying to force his father's hand upon the other "candidate."

The older son, Manasseh, was the one everyone felt deserved this appointment as the heir to the birthright—a high post in the nation called Israel. Jacob rejected Joseph's rebuke and insisted that he knew what he was doing. The one expected to receive the blessing did not get what he "deserved," but the younger son—the one who was not expected to be appointed as leader—received the authority to rule.

So again, perhaps the Torah reading of the week

leading up to the swearing in of a new leader hints at something. Perhaps it shows that the person no one expected to win the election is the one God has chosen for this time. It's like there was another unexpected switch of the blessings—maybe even at the last minute—leaving the one who felt deserving of it rejected and dejected. The recipient of the blessing was Ephraim: born in Egypt and privileged to live in Joseph's palace and associate with the wealthy leaders of Egypt. His name meant "fruitful" even though, according to Joseph, they were in the land of affliction (Genesis 41:52).

The blessing placed upon Ephraim and the circumstances surrounding that blessing might hint at something that is important to us as Americans. In spite of the affliction and oppression of Egypt, God is still able to raise up a leader whose name means "fruitful." In spite of a system that is overseen by pharaohs who don't know the one, true God, the LORD has switched the blessings to the one he has chosen. Again, time will tell if this scenario plays out the way it seems to hint it will.

In that section of Scripture referred to above, there exists another "clue" in regards to the rise of Donald Trump. Prior to Jacob's departing, he began to bless his twelve sons as he leaned on his staff. What is called a blessing ends up sounding more like prophecies pronounced upon the twelve tribes of Israel, in fact telling them what would befall them in the "last days" (Genesis 49:1). Among those twelve sons was Gad, a tribe that did not cross the Jordan River but inherited land on the east side of the river. Jacob predicted, "Gad; a troop shall overcome him, but he shall overcome in the end" (Genesis 49:19).

The Hebrew word "troop" here is *geduwn* and refers to a crowd of men, especially soldiers. The root of this word is from *gadad*, which means not just a crowd but *a crowd that is pressing into a person as if to cut them off or to harm them.* I would say that this is exactly what occurred with Trump. During his entire campaign, the media continually rose against him, cutting him down in every possible manner. Yet in the *end*, he overcame their opposition and won. Once again, this fact was included in the Torah portion being read in the days leading up the inauguration of Trump.

Some of the revelations found in the Torah were portions being read in the days leading up to the week of the inauguration, but what was the parasha being read on the day Trump was sworn in? Ironically—or maybe not—it was the same Torah reading that, eight years before, suggested a new king was coming to power who saw God's people as the enemy. The portion called *Shemot*, or "names" (Exodus 1:1; 6:1), was the parasha being read the very day of Trump's inauguration.

There is much in this narrative, but the central theme focuses on a young man God raised up to demand that the Egyptian leaders "let my people go!" Even as this young man was being reared in the house of Egypt's supreme leader, his government was busily placing heavy loads upon the Hebrews without any benefit to them. When the people finally "cried out," God remembered his covenant with them and raised up an unexpected deliverer—a banished prince of Egypt. When he stepped into his destiny, Moses confronted an evil system—its religion, its politics, and its gods.

THE HAFTARAH READINGS

We covered this earlier, but I want to revisit the portions

of Scripture that accompany the weekly parasha called the haftarah. These are selections taken from the other books of the Tanakh, such as the prophets. The haftarah readings for the week of the inauguration was taken from Isaiah 27:6, 28:13, and 29:22-23. When compared with the reading from Exodus, something interesting may be hinted at as it relates to the Trump presidency. Isaiah 27 begins with: "In that day the LORD with his sore and great and strong sword shall punish Leviathan the piercing serpent, even Leviathan that crooked serpent; and he shall slay the dragon that is in the sea" (Isaiah 27:1).

For those unfamiliar with the term "Leviathan," it is found in the Old Testament in four different passages: Job 41:1, Psalm 74:14, Psalm 104:26, and Isaiah 27:1. The Hebrew word refers to a serpent (some suggest a crocodile) and, in Isaiah's day, was used to allude to the constellation Draco—the dragon. In time, Leviathan also became a symbol for Babylon, the nation that would bring destruction down upon Jerusalem and the Temple. In John the Revelator's vision, the final empire that would control the world for forty-two months is identified as a "dragon with seven heads and ten horns" (Revelation 12:3).

The word *dragon* is used in the 1611 KJV translation a total of thirteen times and is the symbol for Satan himself (see Revelation 12:9; 20:2). Among the early Hebrew believers, the dragon would be equivalent to what Isaiah spoke of when he predicted that God would punish Leviathan. In the same chapter that addresses Leviathan—the haftarah read during the week of Trump's inauguration— we see one word that has repeatedly intrigued believers who are confident Trump has been chosen by God to lead the nation. In Isaiah 27:13 it says: "And it shall come to pass in that day, that the great *trumpet* shall be blown..."

Many well-meaning people have, in my view, stretched things to suggest that Donald Trump's election is somehow connected to the "last trump" spoken of by Paul in 1 Corinthians 15:51-52. This is not the proper way to interpret a verse that deals strictly with the resurrection of the dead in Christ at his return. However, when we are in a prophetic season, and when the Torah reading seems to match circumstances surrounding a national or global event, perhaps there are words and phrases in the text that hint just how the prophetic season will play out.

The context of Isaiah 27 is the redemption of Israel and the end of the exile. The trumpet is sounded for those in exile and captivity to announce their freedom, calling them back to the land of Israel. I do think it is possible that Trump could be a strong and clear voice of support for Israel, maybe even assisting the Jewish nation in settling their disputes with their enemies while still holding on to their biblical inheritance.

In another portion of the haftarah, Isaiah 29, God rebukes the pride of Ephraim, the tribe that received Jacob's blessing. If we are to take away something from this passage that might relate to Trump, perhaps we could say this. I believe that Trump will find it difficult, but absolutely necessary, to commit himself to humility and not allow pride to enter his heart as he serves as president. We shall see.

THE COVENANT WITH DEATH

In Isaiah 28, there may be another warning that we should be aware of. Through the prophet, God addresses the fact that the people of Israel have made a covenant with death and an agreement with hell. To that God says: "And your covenant with death shall be disannulled and your agreement with hell shall not stand; when the over-flowing scourge shall pass through, then you shall be trod-den down by it" (Isaiah 28:18).

Those following the election through the news were shocked at the large numbers of angry people who took to social media, making threats and even calling on some-one to assassinate Trump before he could take office. The weeks following showed no sign of stability, as numerous electors received as many as 50,000 e-mails demanding they change their vote and replace Trump with a different person. Many of these electors related horror stories of being harassed and threatened with death if they followed through with their legal commitment to cast their vote on behalf of the state they represented. Even the ultra-liberal Michael Moore appeared on a televised program suggest-ing that "something could happen before the election," implying a death to then-President-elect Trump.

This is not intended as a prediction because I certain-ly hope no attempt of assault is ever made on Trump, or any other public official for that matter. But because this message was part of the haftarah, it is possible that it "hints" at sinister, such as an assassination attempt against President Trump. That being said, God declared it would be disannulled, so Trump and his team must claim the promise in this verse and believe that "God will disannul it." If there are any devious plots, let us pray that God will cancel out any covenant of death and make the "scourge pass through."

THE HAFTARAH FOR THE SEPHARDIM

Among Israeli Jews, the two main groups are the Sephardic and Ashkenazi. Sometimes, not all the time, these groups have different haftarah readings from week to week. For the week of Trump's inauguration, the Sephardim read a passage taken from Jeremiah. There are some hints contained in several passages that may apply to the president.

The first is God's Word to Jeremiah when the Lord said, "Before I formed you in the womb I knew you" (Jeremiah 1:5). This can be said about every person, but the following verses explain why God marked Jeremiah in particular. We read: "See, I have this day set you over the nations and over the kingdoms, to root out and to pull down, to destroy and to throw down, to build and to plant" (Jeremiah 1:10 (NKJV)).

If there is one verse that totally describes the theme of Trump's presidential campaign, this is it. He promised to "drain the swamp" and root out and pull down the Washington corruption. At the same time, he promised to build up and plant jobs and new companies in the country. The verse is literally addressed to Jeremiah, but the "hint" might apply to some of the elements associated with Trump's election too.

Notice that God also informs Jeremiah that trouble will come from the north like a pot boiling over. Where Israel is concerned, the north alludes to Syria first and then to Russia. Considering some of the news that was swirling about as Trump took office, it will be interesting to see if, or how, Russia interacts with Trump between now and 2020. Time will tell.

Because we are in a major prophetic season and have entered the season of the signs of the time of the end, the readings often "hint" at possible parallels that can or will be repeated (Ecclesiastes 1:9-10). It is time that exposes these possible repetitive patterns, and as believers, we should understand the times and season.

8.

THE DAYS FOR A YEAR THEORY AND ISRAEL'S RESTORATION

The fellow was a moderate Muslim who was expressing his opinion as it relates to the nation of Israel. His comment was, "If it were not for the Christians in Britain and America, there would not be a nation of Israel today, as Western Christians conspired with the Zionists movement from 1917 to 1948 to reform Israel, believing a reformed Israel would be a sign the Christian Messiah—Jesus—would return." Before blowing off this perception as an Islamic slant against Israel, what the fellow said to me that day may actually have a bit of historical merit.

Britain and America are two nations whose faith traditions have been in their early history. They are based upon the Holy Bible and Judeo-Christian principles, including the Torah laws first revealed by divine revelation to the Jews. It is impossible for a Bible-believing Christian to separate himself from the fact that Christianity's roots are planted firmly within the Jewish tree, producing numerous New Covenant branches from the roots. (See Romans

11.) Most biblical prophets were Jews, the original apostles were Jewish, and Christ was born to Mary, a Jewish virgin whose lineage was from the "house of David."

Both America and Britain were also nations whose founders viewed their respective nations as birthed for divine assignments and whose documents and patterns were linked with the same ideas, laws, and patterns of ancient Israel. This American-Israel concept was so intense among various founding fathers and early leaders that the Hebrew language came close to being the official language of the colonies. Several Ivy League universities have Hebrew writing on their seals (including Yale), and drawings of the seals of America's newly formed government were originally sketched by Benjamin Franklin to be the children of Israel crossing the Red Sea. Just as Israel had thirteen tribes, America had thirteen colonies.

The British-Israel link is an early prophetic-centered teaching that circulated for many years called British Israelism. It's a theory expressing that the early people settling in Western Europe, specifically the British, are descendants of not only the lost tribes of Israel. Their royal lineage was also traceable as far back as Judah's son, Zerah, through Tamar (Genesis 38:27-30). In modern times, researchers using DNA, language, and archeology claim to have debunked much of the theory, although there are some arguments in favor of the theory that continue to surface. The strong belief in this theory from the seventeenth century until the reestablishment of Israel in 1948 may help explain why the British Christians studying the Bible, and noting the ancient prophetic writings, played a huge role beginning in 1917. After WWI some British leaders saw an opportunity to partition Palestine and carve out a Jewish homeland.

One of America's main propagators of the American-British Israelite link, called Anglo-Israel Truth (also called "Christian Identity"), was the distinguished evangelist, Dr. Mordecai F. Ham (1877-1961), whose most noted converts were Billy Graham and Grady Wilson. They converted to Christ during Ham's 1935 Charlotte, North Carolina, crusade. Ham's preaching against communism and Zionism was so intent that he was labeled "anti-Semitic" and controversial. Ham publicly taught and wrote that he believed the Scandinavian, German, and Celtic people are the lost tribes of Israel. This Anglo-Israel doctrine was not a modern or late historic theory in the twentieth century, as a statement from 1314 in the Scottish Declaration of Independence at Arbroath Abey compared the Scots' journey to the ancient Israelites:

> "We know from the chronicles and books
> of the ancients gather, that the nation of
> the Scots passing from the greater Scythia
> through the Mediterranean Sea and the
> Pillars of Hercules (Straits of Gibraltar)
> and sojourning in Spain . . . and convey
> there one thousand two hundred years af-
> ter the outgoing of the people of Israel."[19]

In 1590 the French Huguenot Le Loyer wrote on the subject in *The Ten Lost Tribes Found*, teaching that "the Israelites came to and founded the English Isles." As the theory spread, especially among the Protestant writers in the nineteenth centuries, writers such as Ralph Wedgwood in 1813 published a book, *The Book of Remembrance*, theorizing that England was Ephraim. He listed biblical verses on Ephraim, noting that Jacob blessed Ephraim above his older brother, Manasseh, and predicted that "[Ephraim's] seed shall become a multitude of nations" (see Genesis 48:17-20). Those multitude of nations, obviously, would be Gentile nations since at that time (1813) there was not a Jewish state. The idea was that Britain and America were considered the two greatest nations from Ephraim's lineage and a spiritual replacement for Israel, a form of "replacement theology."

As the theory continued expanding and printing presses were rolling this message in theological magazines, books, and newspaper articles, more writers advanced the Anglo-Israel claims. One wrote that Israel had traveled by ship and was linked with the Isle of Erin.[20] Another writing in 1828 taught that the Welsh were descendants of Israel.[21] The 1840s saw a huge resurgence in prophecy preaching and book writing. In 1840, a Scottish Presbyterian minister, Reverend John Wilson M.D., spread the Anglo-Israelite message in a book, *Our Scottish Origin,* using Bible verses and an historical record along with the most recent archeological discoveries. His book was spread far and wide, and his detailed research further advanced the message of Anglo-Israel theory throughout the Protestant world. Eventually, the Anglo-British teaching was received across the sea and gained an adherence among other noted ministers, including Anglican bishops, Methodist ministers, Presbyterians leaders, and Baptists. When men such as Professor Charles Totten of Yale University began expanding the theory, more educated Christians began to accept the idea that the original Anglo people of Britain and America were descendants of ancient Israel.[22]

HENRY GRATTAN GUINNESS

Henry Guinness (1835-1910) was an Irish Protestant minister credited with the evangelical awakening during the Ulster Revival of 1859. Despite consistent persecution, Henry began preaching in Dublin, drawing large crowds to hear his messages. Over time, he won the confidence of judges, Parliament members, college professors, and high-ranking business professionals, many of whom accepted his stunning prophetic theories and interpretations. Near the conclusion of his life, Christians in Wales and England called him "England's greatest prophecy teacher." One of his earliest books was *Approaching the End of the Age*, a popular prophetic book that emphasized the premillennial advent of Christ.

In the preface of *Approaching the End of the Age*, Henry noted the rash of Muhammadan (Islamic) powers and also the papal influence, chiefly the pope and the Roman Catholic Church, which he believed God would soon judge. He, as most Protestants, connected papal influence with the Mystery Babylon the Great, alluded to in the Apocalypse (Revelation 17 and 18), which the apostle John predicted would be burned with fire at the time of the end (Revelation 17:16; 18:8). In his second preface, he wrote the following: "From the day of the accession of Nabonassar, the first king of Babylon, to the day of the fall of Romulus Augustulus, the last emperor of Rome, there lapsed an interval of precisely 1,260 lunar years."[23]

Using the same method God revealed to Ezekiel of exchanging years for days (Ezekiel 4:1-7) and God punishing Israel's forty days of unbelief, forcing them to wander forty years in the wilderness (one year for every day of unbelief—Numbers 14:34), Guinness exchanged the prophetic 1,260 days in the Scripture into years, marking this timeframe as the first half from the first Gentile Empire impacting Jerusalem—from Babylon to Rome, as indicated by the four beasts in Daniel chapter 7. Guinness wrote that there would be another 1,260 years passing, beginning with the rise of Islam in the seventh century to the end of the age, and that the Turkish Mohammadean power that was at the time of writing his book, controlling or influencing three continents, would soon lose their grip on Europe and the Middle East.

In his book, *The Approaching End of the Age, Viewed in the Light of History, Prophecy, and Science*, Guinness noted the longstanding trend of many Christians from the eleventh century forward to his day, which is to interpret the prophetic days in Daniel and Revelation on a "year-day system." He pointed out that many of the earliest reformers, including the Waldens, followers of Wickliff and John Huss, with many reformers of the sixteenth century held this theory with "intense conviction."[24] The author spent much time detailing his belief that Papal Rome was symbolized by John as the woman on the beast in Revelation 17. It's a belief that was promoted among most of the early Protestant reformers, including Martin Luther, John Calvin, John Knox, and others. They all believed the imagery of the harlot was a metaphor for Papal Rome.

Guinness noted on pages 298 and 299 of his book that there were numerous places in the prophetic Scripture, in Daniel (7:25; 9:25-27; 8:14; 12:7, 11, 12) and in Revelation (2:10; 9:5; 9:15; 11:2, 3, 9; 12:6, 14; 13:5) that specify an exact number, usually of days, months, or years, in which the predicted events will begin and conclude. In many of these examples, such as the 1,260, 1,290, and 1,335 days in Daniel, the text indicates that the time frame is specifically "days" and not "years." However, Guinness wrote, "We believe that in all the above fourteen instances, the period of time mentioned is a symbol of another larger period . . ."[25] On page 303 of the same book, he promotes the theory that the numerous dates in apocalyptic Scripture that allude to days should be interpreted as years. Thus, 1,260 days must be understood as 1,260 years, and so forth.

He dated the burning of the Temple in Jerusalem by Nebuchadnezzar (587 A.D.) to Omar capturing Jerusalem (637 A.D.) as 1,260 *lunar* (not solar) years. Since 1,260 is alluded to twice in Revelation (Revelation 11:3; 12:6), Grattan saw a second 1,260 years based upon a lunar calendar that began with Omar's capture of Jerusalem in 637 A.D. and should conclude in the year 1897.

Using this interpretation, Henry made some very bold and, to some, outlandish predictions. He said, "There can be no question that those who live to see this year, 1917, will have reached one of the most momentous of these terminal years of crisis." Years later, prophetic teachers note that numerous and significant prophetic events *did occur* at the conclusion of WWI, in the year 1917, including the signing of the Balfour Declaration.

In summary, this noted teacher, in his day, taught that the time of the end centered near the closing out of the "times of the Gentiles" (Luke 21:24), and once the major Gentile powers become diminished, then the return of Christ would occur. The year 1917 was significant in the early ideas of reforming a Jewish state, and in Luke 21:24, the city of Jerusalem becomes the key to the climax of the time of the Gentiles.

It would be a British military genius, General Edmund Allenby, who in 1917 liberated Palestine and Jerusalem from 400 years of Turkish occupation. During the same year, a unique declaration, the Balfour Declaration, was signed on November 2, 1917, by Lord Balfour, a prominent political Zionist leader, which encouraged a national homeland for Jews in Palestine. This declaration was a recompense given on behalf of a Jewish chemist, Chaim Weizmann, for assisting the allies during WWI by inventing a substance to be used as gunpowder and thus helping the British win the war. For his efforts, Chaim Weismann was asked what he desired, and he suggested a homeland for the Jewish people, leading to the declaration.

EXCHANGING DAYS FOR YEARS

Throughout the nineteenth century, especially in the 1800s, it was common among some scholars and prophecy students to take the prophetic numbers found in Daniel and Revelation and exchange the days into years. The numbers commonly used included 1,260 (Revelation 11:3), 1,290 (Daniel 12:11), 1,335 (Daniel 12:12), and even 666 (Revelation 13:18). In each of these four references, Daniel and John both indicate the time frames are "days" and certainly not years. However, in the Bible there are examples of days being exchanged for years.

This concept has its roots in the Scripture indicating that "one day with God is as a thousand years and a thousand years is as one day" (2 Peter 3:8). This verse indicates that since God dwells in eternity, time is insignificant to him. The idea of a year representing a day first appears with Israel spying out the promised land for forty days. After returning, ten spies doubted they could possess the land while Joshua and Caleb argued it was possible (Numbers 13 and 14). In anger for Israel's unbelief, God

demanded Israel to remain in the desert for forty years—
one year for every day, they doubted, until the unbelieving
generation eventually died off, allowing their children to
inherit the land:

> "But as for you, your carcasses shall fall
> in this wilderness. And your sons shall be
> shepherds in the wilderness forty years,
> and bear the brunt of your infidelity,
> until your carcasses are consumed in the
> wilderness. According to the number of
> the days in which you spied out the land,
> forty days, for each day you shall bear
> your guilt one year, namely forty years,
> and you shall know my rejection" (Num-
> bers 14:32-35).

A second example is when the Lord instructed Ezekiel
to lie on his left side for 390 days, representing the 390
years of the house of Israel's iniquity. Ezekiel was after-
ward told to lie forty days on his right side, representing
the forty years of Judah's iniquity (see Ezekiel 4:1-7). This
illustrates twice that when God was displeased, or his people are in sin and unbelief, he exchanged punishment cycles from days to years.

Perhaps the most noted day-year exchange is concealed in Daniel's seventy "weeks" prophecy. When we in
the West use the term "weeks," everyone pictures a week
of days. However, in Daniel 9, the seventy weeks determined for the Jews, Israel, and Jerusalem is seventy weeks
of years, or 490 years, and not weeks of days, 490 days. In
Daniel 9:27, the future man of sin, the Antichrist, "confirms a covenant with many for one week, then breaks

covenant in the middle of the week." This again is *seven years*, not a *seven-day* treaty as indicated centuries later in John's writing. He reveals to the reader that the seven-year tribulation is 1,260 days for the first half and 1,260 days for the second half (Revelation 11:3; 12:6), or seven years in length.

A fourth example is located in Daniel chapter 4 when King Nebuchadnezzar dreamt an angel descended from heaven, cutting down a beautiful, fruitful tree, leaving only the stump with roots in the ground. A word from heaven was heard instructing the angel to pass over the stump "seven times." These "seven times" were a warning of *seven years*, during which the king would suffer a mental breakdown. Thus, the phrase "times" in Aramaic is *'iddan*, corresponding to a *set time*, and in the context of Daniel 4:16, the "seven times" refers to seven years. Daniel chapter 4 narrates the beginning and ending of King Nebuchadnezzar's seven-year mental breakdown and how the king lived like a wild animal in the wilderness for seven years. Thus, "seven times" is not seven *days* but seven *years*. It became quite common during many centuries for prophetic ministers to exchange the *days for years* in the apocalyptic books of Daniel and Revelation, and in retrospect, many of Henry Guinness' predictions did come to pass on or near the time frames of his predictions.

AMAZING PREDICTIONS FROM THE YEAR-DAY THEORY

In 1896, Theodor Herzl, the spokesman for the Zionist movement, published a book titled *The Jewish State*. The content expressed the dream for the Jewish people to have their own independent state. At that time, there was a rise in Zionism, an ideological movement inspiring Jews to use whatever influence was necessary to make preparations and political plans for a future Jewish homeland. In 1898, it was predicted that within *fifty years* (one Jubilee) a Jewish state would exist. To the amazement of the world, exactly fifty years later, in 1948, Israel was reborn, and David Ben-Gurion announced in Tel-Aviv that the new Jewish state was called Israel. Like a tree blossoming after a long winter, the flowers of a Jewish state were blooming in the spring.

In 1886, ten years before Herzl wrote his book, Reverend W. B. Godbey compiled and printed an interesting commentary on the book of Revelation, which expressed an interesting theory that became widespread. He dated the "Gentile Age" beginning with the Babylonian invasion of Jerusalem in 587 B.C. His interest was to determine just how long the "Times of the Gentiles" would continue, noting that when this Gentile control of Jerusalem ends, and the city is in the hands of Israel, then the return of the Lord occurs thereafter (see Luke 21:24-28). Godbey noted there were actually three different chronologies marking time: the *lunar* calendar, which uses 354 days a year; the *prophetic* calendar, which had in the past been used in parts of Europe (consisting of 360 days a year or twelve months of thirty days each); and the standard *solar* calendar, which consisted of 365 days making a year. This was the time required for the earth to make one full revolution around the sun.[26]

Beginning with these three different calendars, Godbey then observed a Scripture in Leviticus 26:18, which warned that God would allow "seven times more punishment" for Israel's disobedience and lack of repentance, if they continued to reject his laws. Godbey added numbers on the lunar, prophetic, and solar cycles, multiplying each of the three calendar numbers by seven, which is the number of "time punishment" God assigned for Israel's sins. Using the day-for-a-year theory, which in his day was a popular method of prophetic interpretation, below are the numbers after multiplying the three calendar days by seven.

THE TYPE OF CALENDAR	THE CALENDAR DAYS MULTIPLIED BY SEVEN	THE TOTAL DAYS INTO YEARS
The lunar calendar	354 days multiplied seven times is 2,478	2,478
The prophetic calendar	360 days multiplied seven times is 2,520	2,520
The solar calendar	365 days multiplied seven times is 2,555	2,555

His desire was to find a beginning point in history when these "years" could be calculated and totaled to the time of the end. After researching, he pinpointed the date 587 B.C., which was taught as the year when Jerusalem fell into the hands of the Babylonians, or the beginning of the fullness of Gentile control over Jerusalem. Once he established a beginning point at 587 B.C., he moved forward in time by adding the number of years based upon each calendar.

The lunar calendar from 587 B.C. moving forward 2,478 years came to the Gregorian year of 1891. The prophetic calendar from 587 B.C. moving forward 2,520 years ended at the year 1933. The third calendar, the solar, moved from 587 B.C. forward 2,555 years ending at 1968. Oddly, time proved that there were significant events occurring during each of these dates. In 1891, a case was being made for the Zionist Movement, which as alluded to previously, worked behind the scenes, assisting years later in reestablishing Israel as a Jewish state. The 1933 date marks the rise of Adolf Hitler, who would lead the world into war and initiate the horrible Holocaust against the Jews. The third date, 1968, was unique as it marked one year after the Six Day War (June 1967) when Israel was able to reunite Jerusalem and capture land that was preciously promised them through the Abrahamic and Davidic covenants. Thus, by 1968, the Gentile dominion over Israel and Jerusalem had concluded.

To me, the most unique prediction during his 1896 calculations was a statement he made related to the Muslim conquest of Palestine. He predicted it would soon come to a conclusion. Using Daniel 8:13-14, a prophecy concerning the sanctuary (in Jerusalem) being cleansed, he again turned the "days" into "years" and came to this conclusion. "The Muslims conquered Palestine and captured Jerusalem in 637 A.D., driving Christians out. Daniel says they will hold it twelve hundred and sixty years . . . (1,260). Hence you see, according to the prophecies, the Mohammedan (Islamic) power in Palestine will fall in 1897."

Godbey wrote: "When it falls in Palestine, there is no alternative but for the Holy Land to pass into Christendom." He also predicted the following:

> "I am exceedingly hopeful the Holy Land will pass into the British Empire. This becomes more than probable since Baron Rothschild is a son of Abraham, an officer in the British Government, the richest man in the world holds a mortgage on all that country . . . The moment that Turkdom falls, Jerusalem and the Holy Land will pass into Christendom. Then that country will turn it over to the Jews, its

rightful owners . . . this notable event will
be a sunburst on the Christian world."[27]

The date 1897 came and went without the Turks in
Palestine departing from Jerusalem. However, twenty
years later, in December 1917, the Turks did hand over
the keys of Jerusalem's gates to a Christian, British General
Edmund "The Bull" Allenby. The British, who had
established a mandate in Palestine, ended their mandate
at midnight on May 14, 1948, upon which time the nation
of Israel was recognized, and the Jewish homeland
reborn. Godbey's prediction came true; the Christians
would turn the land over to the rightful owners, the Jews.

The British were blessed with numerous prophecy writers,
ministers, and prophetic researchers in the early and
late eighteen and nineteenth centuries. They had written
about British involvement in reestablishing a homeland
for the Jews. Their articles were printed in papers and
spoken in lecture halls that were filled with curious seekers
of prophetic insight. Their books were often read by leaders
in the British Parliament. The seeds of prophecy were
planted by the very nation of people whose ancestors gave
us the 1611 King James translation of the English Scriptures.
The British prophetic emphasis paved the way for
the reestablishment of Israel and a Jewish homeland.

One more note. In 1917, when the British intelligence
were discussing how to capture Jerusalem from the Turks,
it was noted that Isaiah said that, "As birds flying, the *Lord*
would defend Jerusalem and deliver it and passing over
he would preserve it" (Isaiah. 31:5). After reading this
verse, the idea came to fly British scout planes over Jerusalem
and drop leaflets demanding the Turks to surrender,
which the British did. A story emerged that when Allen-

by's name was written in the Turkish language on the leaflet, the Turks, who were quite superstitious, read it as "Allah-Nebi," meaning "God's prophet." Allenby walked into Jerusalem without firing a single shot by "flying over the city like birds." The previous verse in Isaiah 31 speaks of the "lion and the young lion that will . . . come down to fight for Mount Zion." One of the main national symbols of Britain was, and is, a lion. The symbol on the coat of arms for England is three gold lions. Thus, many in Britain saw the capturing and liberating of Jerusalem as a direct fulfillment of Isaiah's ancient prediction found in Isaiah 31:4-5.

ISAIAH'S "ONE DAY" PROPHECY

On May 14, 1948, when the official announcement was made that the Jews now had a homeland named Israel, scholars pointed out Isaiah 66:8: "Who hath heard such a thing? Who hath seen such things? Shall the earth be made to bring forth in one day? Or shall a nation be born at once? For as soon as Zion travailed, she brought forth her children."

Travail is a word used by biblical prophets indicating the serious trials or tribulations the Jewish people would experience at times, especially from enemies set on their destruction. In this passage, "Zion" travails to bring forth the nation (children), which many prophetic scholars believe alludes to the travail of the Holocaust. Note the prophet indicated this would occur in "one day," or "at once." The one day was May 14, 1948; however, the Hebrew word "once" (KJV) is unique, as here it is *pa'am*, which carried several meanings and can be translated as *second time* (Genesis 43:10; Nahum 1:9) or *two* (Genesis 27:36) in the KJV. Israel was dispersed twice—once during the Babylonian siege and the second by the Roman Tenth Legions. Their restoration in 1948 was the *second time* they were restored! Isaiah predicted this when he wrote, "And it shall come to pass in that day, that the Lord shall set his hand again the second time to recover the remnant of his people, which shall be left, from Assyria, and from Egypt, and from Pathros, and from Cush, and from Elam, and from Shinar, and from Hamath, and from the islands of the sea" (Isaiah 11:11).

The *one* Jewish movement that historians identify as the main influence that pressured world leaders to recognize the Jewish state was the Zionist movement. Statistics reveal that two-thirds of Jews living in Europe before WWI were killed during the Holocaust (1938 to 1945), including 1.5 million children. One verse stood out after the Holocaust, recorded 2,600 years ago by Zechariah: "And I will bring the third part through the fire, and will refine them as silver is refined, and will try them as gold is tried: they shall call on my name, and I will hear them: I will say, It is my people: and they shall say, The LORD is my God" (Zechariah 13:9 (KJV)). The one-third can allude to those who survived the Holocaust.

HOW SHOULD THE NUMBERS BE INTERPRETED?

The question then arises: How should the prophetic numbers in Daniel and Revelation be interpreted? Should we equate a day for a year in these examples or remain firm that these are literal days only? The main danger of exchanging the days to years is that a person could distort the true meaning of the prophecies, and if their starting point for adding the years is wrong, then their entire theory falls apart. It is best to always point to the interpretation within the text, as Daniel and John both indicate these time frames are "days" (Daniel 12:11, 12; Revelation 11:3, 6, 9; 12:6). In Hebrew the word "day" is *yom*, and it is always interpreted as a literal day, or from a sunrise to sunset. In Greek, the word day is *hemera*, meaning a literal day. It is divided by the Jews in Christ time between twelve hours and twelve hours totaling twenty-four hours (John 11:9). It is clear the primary meaning of these time frames is intended to be days. However, it can be confirmed that, at times, the word "week" in our 1611 English translation, in Hebrew, refers to a week of years and not days, as in the case when Jacob worked an additional "week" (Genesis 29:27-28) to gain Rachel as his wife. In reality, this was seven years (Genesis 29:27-28). The Daniel 9:27 prediction that the covenant is confirmed for "one week" is, in reality, seven years.

This is where a careful and clear system of biblical interpretation must be established and maintained. However, to explain the amazing accuracy of equating a day for a year among some of the older noted prophetic teachers is difficult for a literalist who would never use the day for a year system. I do not believe it should be the interpretation of the text, but herein we have the concept of prophetic layers and how prophecy is multi-dimensional. A prime example is the fall of Lucifer. We know this created cherub was perfect until iniquity was found in him, and in an attempt to overthrow God, he was expelled from heaven along with a third of the angelic host. This fact is clear in the context of Revelation 12, especially verse four: "And his tail drew the third part of the stars of heaven, and did cast them to the earth" (Revelation 12:4).

This initial interpretation refers to mid-tribulation when Michael the archangel will expel Satan and his angels from the second heaven to the earth. However, it can be deduced from this passage that Satan has a third of the angels with him, and these angels would have been removed at the same time he too was cast out of heaven (see Isaiah 14:12-15; Ezekiel 28:13-17; Luke 10:18; Revelation 12:1-4). The verse reveals a future event but parallels the original expulsion of Satan from heaven (Luke 10:18).

John Walvoord, former president of Dallas Theological Seminary, listed several important hermeneutical rules for interpreting biblical prophecy. The first is, words are to be understood in their normal, natural sense unless there is firm evidence in the context that the word is used in some other sense. Second, each statement should be interpreted in its context of what is written. The text must be seen in the historical and cultural context of that day and time.[28]

When ministers preach the Word of God, I have noted they preach the story as historical fact and then often flow into comparing the events of the past to parallel a similar situation today. Some ministers will also paint an allegorical comparison, or use the imagery as a type, shadow, or pattern. In this case, one verse is expounded in many senses. The Song of Solomon is a true love story, and yet it conceals the message of Christ and his bride. As time moves forward I am certain that fresh insight will flourish from the ancient prophecies of the Bible.

9.

PROPHECIES CONCEALED ON THE JEWISH CALENDAR

The time of the creation of Adam in Genesis 1:27 to the birth of Abraham, the father of the Hebrew people who formed Israel (Genesis 11:26) is exactly 1,948 years. This is evident when reading the Genesis genealogies, giving the age of each father when his first son was born: We begin in Genesis 5:3 through 11:26.

5:3	Adam to Seth	− 130 years
5:6	Seth to Enos	− 105 years
5:9	Enos to Kenan	− 90 years
5:12	Kenan to Mahalaleel	− 70 years
5:15	Mahalaleel to Jared	− 65 years
5:18	Jared to Enoch	− 162 years
5:21	Enoch to Methuselah	− 65 years
5:25	Methuselah to Lamech	− 187 years
5:28	Lamech to Noah	− 182 years
5:32	Noah to Shem[29]	− 500 years

11:10	Shem to Arphaxad	
	(2 years after flood)	– 2 years
11:12	Arphaxad to Salah	– 35 years
11:14	Salah to Eber	– 30 years
11:16	Eber to Peleg	– 34 years
11:18	Peleg to Reu	– 30 years
11:20	Reu to Serug Peleg	– 32 years
11:22	Serug to Nahor	– 30 years
11:24	Nahor to Terah	– 29 years
11:26	Terah to Abram	– 70 years
17:1-24	Abraham to Isaac	– 100 years

1,948 years

The apostle Paul described the first man created as "the first Adam" and called Jesus Christ the "last Adam" (1 Corinthians 15:45). Time is the Christian world, and the Gentile world is generally computed and gauged with the birth of Christ. The years before the birth are dates B.C., or "before Christ," and the years following the birth are called A.D., the abbreviation for the Latin phrase *Anno Domini*, meaning "In the year of our Lord." Thus, the birth of Christ was the dividing point of world history. 1 B.C. identifies time before Christ's birth, and 1 A.D. marks the beginning of his birth (although there is controversy concerning the exact year of Christ's birth in Bethlehem). The point is, from 1 A.D., with the appearing of the last Adam, to the very year when the natural descendants of Abraham saw their nation restored as a nation among nations is 1,948 years, or May 14, 1948. On this day at midnight, the British Mandate over Palestine ended, and a nation was carved out of the land known as Palestine and given the ancient biblical name, Israel. A precious man named David Ben-Gurion read a Declaration of Independence, formally establishing a homeland for the Jews. It was the fifth of Iyar on the Jewish calendar in the Jewish year 5707. The name Iyar is a Babylonian name given to the month that usually falls in May each year. In the Bible, it is called "the second month" or "*codesh haziv*," meaning "the month of shining or blossoming." This is interesting since Israel, a nation that was dead in the eyes of the world since 70 A.D., was now emerging from the darkness of the Holocaust, rising like dry bones from their graves. The prophet Isaiah predicted that the deserts in Israel would "blossom like a rose" (Isaiah 35:1). The month of Iyar falls between the month of Passover redemption (Nissan) and the month (Sivan) of revelation when Moses received the law on Mount Sinai. The second year Israel was in the wilderness, it was in the month of Iyar when the tabernacle was complete and Israel began their ministry in God's presence at the tabernacle in the wilderness (Exodus 40:17).

The month of Iyar is mentioned fourteen times in the Old Testament. It was in the second month that the flood of Noah was unleashed on the world (Genesis 7:11). It was also in the second month that the flood waters dried on the earth (Genesis 8:14). Thus, in Iyar, the flood brought destruction and in the same month introduced restoration. Israel departed from Egypt and found themselves in the wilderness on the fifteenth day of the second month (Exodus 16:1). This would parallel May 15th, when Israel, 3,500 years later, was restored to their promised land, yet found themselves, as Joshua did, surrounded by hostile nations who fought against Israel's return. It was also in the second month when Moses, Israel's leader, took a major census of the nation and the people "declared their pedigrees" (Numbers 1:18). There were 600,000 men of war who departed from Egypt with their families, and amazingly, in 1948, there were 600,000 Jews in Israel that year, many immigrating back to the land of their father, Abraham. Another great prophetic event occurred on June 7, 1967, which was Iyar 28 on the Jewish calendar. It was when Israeli troops liberated the Temple Mount, and Israeli troops planted an Israeli flag just above the Western Wall. The flag was soon removed to prevent a political conflict with Islamic authorities who oversaw the two Islamic mosques on the sacred mountain.

THE PASSOVER SHINI AND IYAR

The first Passover in Exodus 12 transpired on the Hebrew calendar on the fourteenth day of the first month, called Nissan today or Abib (Exodus 13:4) in Moses' time. This day was marked as Passover, the first of seven of Israel's sacred festivals (Deuteronomy 16). Three of the seven required all men over twenty years of age to ascend to Jerusalem and celebrate. What is unusual is that God established a second Passover, called the *Passover Sheni* (*sheni* meaning "second"). The second day of the week (Monday) is called Yom Sheni in Hebrew, thus the Passover Sheni refers to a second Passover that was provided for any person who had touched a dead body. He was required to bury a corpse or was on a far journey away from the land and could not celebrate the first Passover. These individuals were given the option of celebrating Passover the following month, which happened to be "the fourteenth day of the second month (Iyar)" and in the fire became the same day as when Israel was officially restored as a nation—May 14, 1948! The Passover was a memorial reminding Israel of her deliverance from the hands of her enemies and her day of redemption. The Hebrew verb for "redeem" is *gaal*, and the central meaning is to "regain possession of by payment" or to "buy something back that was lost." Following the Holocaust, the Jewish people regained possession of the land and took back what had been lost in 70 A.D. This began the seasons of redemption and was a rabbinical harbinger that the season of the signs of the Messianic era had begun. This would initiate Israel's greatest and ultimate redemption.

Not only is this second Passover celebrated on the fourteenth of Iyar, but another minor celebration is commemorated on the twenty-eighth day of the month of Iyar called "Jerusalem Day." This day recalls the Six Day War in which Israel conquered Jerusalem, reuniting the city as the spiritual and political capital of Israel. The first day of Iyar was the same month when Solomon began construction on the first Temple (1 Kings 6:1), and on the exact same day, hundreds of years later, Ezra began constructing the second Temple (Ezra 3:8). Since Passover is the season linked to Israel's redemption, this second Passover, Shini, is God giving a second chance to his people. Isaiah wrote that "The Lord will set his hand again the second time to recover the remnant of his people, which shall be left, from Assyria, and from Egypt, and from Pathros, and from Cush, and from Elam, and from Shinar and from the islands of the sea" (Isaiah 11:11).

From 740 to 722 B.C., the Assyrians captured the ten northern tribes of Israel, scattering these Israelites among the Gentile nations. However, Judah and Benjamin, the southern tribes, remained in Judea and prospered in the land. This dispersion was not the fulfillment of Isaiah's prediction since tens of thousands remained in the land after the Assyrian assault. Israel was, however, dispersed twice—the first during the seventy years of Babylonian captivity when the armies of Babylon destroyed Jerusalem and the Temple, seizing the sacred vessels. The second dispersion, and the worst, was the Roman destruction of Jerusalem in 70 A.D., leaving the city in smothering ruins. The Jews then were without a homeland until 1948. Thus, as Isaiah predicted, the Jews would return from numerous nations back to the land. In history, this prophecy would have begun its fulfillment in May (Iyar) 1948 and has continued to this day.

HEALING ISRAEL IN THE MONTH OF IYAR

It was during the month of Iyar when the people of Israel found themselves in the wilderness, unable to find fresh, drinkable water. Moses cast a tree into the bitter waters, turning them into refreshing water. It was during this time that God provided a healing covenant to Israel, promising, "I am the Lord that healeth thee" (Exodus 15:26). In Hebrew, the individual letters for Iyar can form an acronym for "I am the Lord Your Healer!" Thus, Iyar is marked with the theme of restoration, blossoming, and healing, all three of which occurred when Israel was restored as a nation on May 14, 1948!

A second interesting prophetic nugget linked with the year 1948 is found in the Jewish calendar. The Jewish calendar in 1948 was the year 5708. The Jewish holidays always fall on the same days on their calendar; however, the secular months may vary. For example, Passover is always the fourteenth day of the first month; however, the actual month could be March or April, depending upon the calendar.

The Jewish calendar is based upon three forms of cosmic activity: the rotation of the earth on its axis (twenty-four hours, making one day), the moon's revolution around the earth (twenty-nine and one-half days, making a month), and the earth moving around the sun (365.25 days, making a year). The calendar used in Western nations and most of the world averages one year as 365.25 days, adding leap years to maintain a correct solar calendar. To maintain a proper Jewish religious calendar, each year has either twelve or thirteen months to ensure the seven festivals remain in their proper seasonal alignment—three in the spring, one in early summer, and three in the fall month of Tishri.

On the Christian calendar, there has been slightly over 6,000 years from the creation of Adam to this present age. The Jewish reckoning of time is actually about 225 years short of our 6,000-year dating of biblical history. However, the Jewish calendar dates reveal some interesting prophetic insights.

THE PROPHECY CONCEALED IN 5708

One of the rabbinical methods of discovering prophecies concealed in the Torah is to count the verses in the Torah and align the verses with the Jewish year to see if the actual verse conceals a prediction that occurred on the Jewish year. This was believed to be a method used in the Roman era by the Essenes, a community of men living near the Dead Sea at a village called Qumran. We read:

> "The Essenes had the gift of prophecy.
> They had knowledge to give numerical
> values to letters. They exchanged certain

letters with opposite letters. They could not only predict the details of a sacred writing, but could determine the exact time of the prophecy fulfillment with astute accuracy. Rarely if ever, did the prediction prove wrong."[30]

When employing this particular approach, a researcher must take the Gregorian calendar year and exchange it for the Jewish year, always remembering that the Jewish calendar transitions in the fall months, whereas the Gregorian calendar transitions at midnight, December 31st. For example, the Gregorian calendar 2016 aligned on the Jewish year 5777, 2017 falls on the Jewish year 5778, and so forth. The Torah scroll itself has no chapter or verse headings, but in a printed Torah book, the chapters and verses were added centuries ago. The chapter divisions separate the different narratives, and the verses separate individual thoughts or statements within the chapters.

While there are a few variations, the number of verses in each of the five books in the Torah are:

Genesis	− 1,533
Exodus	− 1,213
Leviticus	− 859
Numbers	− 1,288
Deuteronomy	− 959

5,852 total verses

When exchanging the year 1948 (May 1948) to the Jewish year, 1948 was the year 5708. It was noted that when counting the verses in the first five books of the

Bible (the Torah), coming to the 5,708th verse, the passage appears to encode a prediction that correlates to the year 1948. The 5,708th verse is Deuteronomy 30:5, which reads: "And the Lord your God will bring thee into a land which thy fathers possessed and thou shalt possess it and he will do thee good and multiply thee above thy fathers" (KJV).

This verse was a direct promise from God predicting Israel's return to the land after being dispersed among the Gentile nations! This regathering was after the seven-year Holocaust (1938-1945) as God performed his promise, opening the doors to Palestine for the Jews to return to their promised land, eventually conferring upon the natural descendants of Abraham their original name, Israel. The 5,708th Torah verse equated to the Jewish year of its fulfillment.

Another example can be found in the year 1952, which would match the Jewish calendar year of 5712. The 5,712th verse of the Torah, found in Deuteronomy 30:9, also holds an amazing prediction that links with events occurring in 1952. We read: "And the Lord thy God will make thee plenteous in every work of thine hand, in the fruit of thy body, and in the fruit of thy cattle, and in the fruit of thy land, for good: for the Lord will again rejoice over thee for good, as he rejoiced over thy fathers" (KJV).

It was in the early 1950s when the "father" of modern Israel, David Ben-Gurion, initiated a significant agricultural project designed to make the dry, desolate wilderness (deserts) of Israel produce much-needed vegetation. Today, Israel is so successful that the entire desert region is blossoming, and during winter months, the desert is cultivated: farmers harvest fruits and vegetables that are shipped around the world. Isaiah predicted that Israel would "blossom and fill the world with fruit" (Isaiah 27:6). The once brown, dusty landscape is now carpeted with green vegetation and miles of tents protecting banana trees from the burning rays of the sun, spreading across the landscape.

This is another example of taking the Jewish calendar and viewing specific Torah verses, revealing hints of future events listed within the text itself. This is another amazing proof of the inspiration of the Word of God. The evidence revealed through research indicated there are amazing hints and clues of prophetic insight linked with biblical numbers and Hebraic forms of interpretation.

10.

PROPHECIES IN THE DEAD SEA SCROLLS

The Dead Sea is a body of bluish-green water, over 1,300 feet below sea level, known as the lowest spot on earth. Located on the western side, just off the northern end of the sea, are the stone ruins of a once-thriving village called Qumran. Most scholars believe a community of men called the Essenes lived on this plateau at the base of the Judean wilderness, separating themselves from worldly pleasures, concentrating on study, and scribing messages on parchments, including copying numerous books of the Bible (from the Old Testament). Qumran is noted as the site of the greatest discoveries of early scrolls in the world. What makes this scroll-find so significant is the *timing* of their discovery. Numerous parchments were hidden in large clay jars, concealed from the public in caves scattered throughout the surrounding area. The initial discovery was made in the spring of 1947, almost one year prior to Israel being restored as a nation. Eleven caves were excavated from 1947 to 1956. The approximate 200 individual men believed to have lived at Qumran were thought to be either spiritual separatists called Essenes or perhaps a group of men linked to the priesthood in Jerusalem. Rome's political occupation and Jerusalem's spiritual corruption among the temple priests motivated this remnant of holy men to separate themselves in the desert, awaiting a Messianic figure to deliver Israel and defeat evil.

An initial discovery of the scrolls—many dating back to before the destruction of the Temple in 70 A.D.—by a shepherd boy in 1947 stunned the academic world of biblical and historical scholars. And later, after translating the scroll of Isaiah, the scroll discovery confirmed Isaiah's translation from the Masoretic text.

The scrolls fall into two categories—biblical and non-biblical—and they are written in the three main languages of the day: Hebrew, Greek, and Aramaic. These separatists were most definitely interested in Bible prophecy, especially any predictions related to the "last days" and the "time of the end." The Essenes were familiar with the writings of the major biblical prophets and included in some of their commentaries predictions from Daniel, Jeremiah, and Ezekiel not found in the Bible.

The book of Daniel was an intriguing manuscript, as within his prophecies the prophet gives specific timeframes in which prophetic events would befall the world. This includes "time, times and a half" or forty-two months (Daniel 12:7), 1,290 days (Daniel 12:11), and 1,335 days (Daniel 12:12). Daniel's apocalyptic visions and dreams were significant to the Qumran community, as no fewer than eight manuscripts were discovered in three of the eleven Qumran caves.

Scholars and researchers have summed up the Dead

Sea literature at Qumran as a "Messianic elite retreating or 'separating' into the wilderness as per Isaiah 40:3 'make a straight way in the wilderness for our God.'" This elite inhabited "desert camp" where they were preparing to be joined by the angels, which they called "the Heavenly Host," is what appears to be, in their writings, a final apocalyptic Holy War against evil on earth.[31]

PROPHETIC IMAGERY USED

Much of the imagery in numerous scrolls paints a scene of an end-time battle between the sons of darkness and the children of light. In numerous scrolls the Qumran scribes transcribed phrases also used among biblical prophets and later found in the book of Revelation, a vision by John recorded approximately twenty-seven years after the destruction of Qumran by the Romans in 68 A.D. In Qumran literature there is a "righteous teacher" clashing with a "wicked priest" in an apocalyptic conflict. Certain passages use the phrase of the "cup of the Lord's divine anger," the same word penned by Isaiah in Isaiah 51:22 and John in Revelation 14:10.

Three titles (names) are found throughout the scrolls, including *Bela'* (a king from Edom and a Benjaminite king), *Balaam*, the prophet in the book of Numbers who taught the Moabites how to provoke God's anger by making Israel sin, and the name *Belial*. This name is believed to be the last name given to the devil. The apostle Paul in 2 Corinthians 6:15 uses the name Belial when speaking of evil. This name is also found in the Old Testament (Judges 19:22; 20:13; 1 Sam. 1:16) and is used of worthless and evil men.

The Daniel imagery, found in his vision of the four

kingdoms, is repeated on a Qumran scroll fragment and presents a different perspective. In the Qumran fragment, the King of Babylon (either Nebuchadnezzar or Belshazzar) sees a vision of four trees. In the vision, each tree represents four different kingdoms that rule in succession on earth. Nothing is known of who these four represent, with the exception of the first, which is Babylon. Among biblical prophets, trees are used to represent kingdoms (see Ezekiel 17 and 31 and Zechariah 11:2). King Nebuchadnezzar experienced a troubling dream of a huge tree that was cut down to a stump by an angel, who then passed over the stump seven times (Daniel 4:16). Daniel interpreted this as a prophetic warning dream, indicating the tree represented the kingdom of Babylon, and God was going to remove Nebuchadnezzar ("hew down"— Daniel 4:14) for a period of seven years. In this particular Qumran scroll fragment, there are four angels connected to the four trees. Since Daniel revealed four distinct beasts in chapters 7 and 8, and these four trees represent kingdoms, this alleged vision given to the King of Babylon may refer to the four "trees" of Babylon, Media-Persia, Greece, and Rome.

A Prophecy Discovered at Masada

Located 1,300 feet on the west side of the Dead Sea is a rugged, high mountain, flat on the top, that holds the 2,000-year-old ruins of an ancient Jewish fortress called Masada. The name means "mountain fortress." This high mountain rises 820 feet on the east side and 600 feet on the west, and on top are twenty-six acres of solid rock and ruins with numerous cisterns for collecting rainwater. This almost-impregnable fortress was one of the final strongholds where Jewish zealots and their families, re-sisting Roman occupation, held out against the Romans. They did this until a large man-made dirt ramp was built, allowing the Romans, after seven years, to breech the des-ert stronghold, only to be shocked when finally entering the stronghold town. They had viewed the bodies of 960 Jewish rebels and their families who had committed sui-cide to prevent being captured and taken prisoner by the Romans.

I have visited Masada numerous times, and my Jewish tour guides have masterfully explained details of the exca-vations and discoveries at Masada. Beginning in October 1963 and then in April 1965, Masada was excavated by a team of Israeli archeologists led by the noted archeologist Yigael Yadin, who excavated and unearthed 98 percent of the fortress. He exposed Herod's palace and a Jewish syn-agogue considered the earliest synagogue known. Amaz-ing discoveries were found among the ruins in numerous locations, including sixteen fragments of scrolls from Genesis, Leviticus, Deuteronomy, Psalms, and Ezekiel. The Ezekiel and Deuteronomy fragments were discov-ered in a pit under the synagogue's floor. Yadin reported, to the amazement of many, that the texts were identical to the text in the Hebrew Bible. This indicated the care-fulness scribes used when copying the biblical scrolls. In all, fourteen scrolls that included biblical, sectarian, and apocryphal verses were discovered.

One Psalms fragment was Psalm 85:6, which asks the question, "Wilt thou not revive us again that thy people may rejoice in thee?" Many believe this was a question asked by the Masada zealots: Would God help them de-feat the Roman occupiers? The Ezekiel fragment found under the synagogue floor was an amazing discovery in light of its prophetic implications. The preserved passage recounts the beginning of Ezekiel 37, the vision of the dry bones that were raised to live again. Rabbis note that this Ezekiel vision predicts that at the end of days, the house of Israel would revive, and Israel would be brought back from their dispersion among the nation to reform a new nation in the very land, Israel, where they were scattered!

What makes this discovery so amazing is its discovery occurred after 1948, after the Holocaust (the dry bones vision of Ezekiel 37), and when Israel was reestablished as a nation, also a theme of the Ezekiel vision. Devout Jews who survived the Holocaust recall how thousands of Jews in concentration camps were so famished, their bodies were thin; they were skeletons overlaid with a thin layer of skin. In his boneyard vision, Ezekiel described a house of "dry bones," only layered with skin that required the breath of God to breathe upon them, raising them from their graves to become a great army (see Ezekiel 37). In the vision, once the bones united, they became a "great army," called Israel (Ezekiel 37:10), and would no longer be two nations (northern and southern kingdom, Ezekiel 37:15-22).

The fragment, according to Yadin, may have been buried under the floor as a kind of *geniza*, a place where scrolls are buried when the ink becomes slightly unreadable, or it may have been hidden by the Zealots under the floor before they came to their deaths. If so, they understood this Ezekiel prediction as a future event in which God would bring Israel back from their enemy's land, raise them up again, and make them a mighty nation and great army. How unique that this small portion of Ezekiel's stunning prophecy was discovered after Israel had returned in 1948 and a few years before Jerusalem would be reunited as one city, as the capital of Israel after a Six Day War in 1967.

THE MYSTERIOUS GABRIEL STONE

During one of my Holy Land tours I was invited to the Israeli museum to see a spectacular stone displayed among thousands of ancient artifacts. It dated back to early civilization and moved forward to the Roman destruction of the Temple. I was quite shocked to see skeletal remains of mammoths discovered at the Jordan River, ancient pottery of all forms, gold and silver coins, crude weapons, and clay, ceramic, and metallic idols that in the past released the disfavor of God upon the rebellious Israelites. Now behind secure glass, they were unable to break their way out to freedom!

On display for a limited time was a large, limestone tablet—three feet in length and about six inches thick, dating back to the first century B.C. (at the time of the second Temple). It contained eighty-seven lines of information from an unknown prophetic writer. The Hebrew script was penned using ink. It was believed to have been discovered on the Jordanian side of the banks of the Dead Sea, somewhat by "accident." It was acquired by Israel and has been translated. There were several places where the Hebrew text is unreadable, but in other places it told of a prophecy involving Jerusalem. The stone tablet predicts "a shaking in heaven and earth" and promises that God would hear the cries of Jerusalem, protecting the city. Perhaps the most astonishing fact is that the writer asks who the messenger is bringing the revelation, and the messenger answers, "I am Gabriel." In Scripture, Gabriel is the angel bringing divine revelation from God. He is seen telling Zechariah he would have a son named "John" who would minister in the power of Elijah. And he reveals to Mary that her son would be called "Jesus" and be the savior of mankind (see Luke 1 and 2). In the biblical narrative, the angel proclaimed to Zacharias, "I am Gabriel" (Luke 1:19).

Called "The Gabriel Stone," the mysterious writer speaks of evil being defeated (line twenty) and the chariots of God surrounding Jerusalem for protection (lines twenty-six and twenty-seven). He writes of three prophet-shepherds God sent to Jerusalem (lines seventy and seventy-five). Line eighty has been translated "In three days the sign will be (given) I am Gabriel."

The line predicting "three days" was translated by a professor with the last name Knohl to read, "By three days—live. I Gabriel command you prince of princes, the dung of rocky crevices." Later at Rice University, Knohl said he had mistranslated the line, and it should read, "In three days the sign will be (given). I am Gabriel." It has been noted that the prediction on the stone may be related to the Messianic expectations that were evident as far back as hundreds of years prior to the advent of Christ. When scholars examined the stone line by line, interpreting words that were clear and speculating about words where letters had faded, it was obvious this stone was in line with specific predictions Gabriel had given to Daniel. The tablet contains elements of war, bloodshed, exile, mourning, and death. The stone is clearly prophetic in nature. Whatever scribe took the effort to write on this large, heavy stone intended that the message be preserved and read in the future.

THE DEAD SEA SCROLLS AND
ISRAEL'S RESTORATION

After secret negotiations, in 1947 when the Dead Sea

Scrolls were privately purchased by a Jewish professor, the man took the scrolls to his home. After unrolling one on his table, he began to look at the amazing writing on the ancient parchments. They had not been viewed by Jewish eyes since before the destruction of the Temple. They had been confined and somehow preserved to be discovered nineteen centuries later. He noted that the date he was viewing the parchment was November 29, 1947. At that very moment, his radio was on as he was listening to the United Nations vote, giving the Jews the right to form a Jewish state in Palestine. Before him were the scrolls that had accurately, and eerily, predicted the return of Israel and the reestablishment of the Jewish people to their homeland. Certainly this was a sign from God!

As more scrolls emerged from their dry, dusty hiding place and were placed under the careful care of professors and scientists, help was needed to open the fragile scrolls, restore fragments, and interpret their messages. Each scroll and individual parchment was numbered, detailing when and where it was found, and given a name: the Isaiah Scroll, the Thanksgiving Scroll, the War Scroll, the Temple Scroll, and one of which a copy had been previously discovered about fifty years prior, The Damascus Document.

THE DAMASCUS DOCUMENT

It was the year 1896. In an old synagogue in Cairo, Egypt, a Jewish man named Solomon Schechter (an American Jewish scholar) made an amazing discovery. While remodeling an old synagogue, he discovered ancient fragments of parchments hidden within the wall, having laid in secret for centuries. After he collected the parchments, a total of thirty bags with thousands of fragments were transferred to Cambridge University. After careful examination and interpreting the information penned on the parchments, Schechter had discovered, among the treasure trove, a tenth-century copy of a first-century document.

The document was dubbed "The Zadok Fragment," named for the faithful high priest in David and Solomon's time (Ezekiel 44:15). The document was first published in 1910 and became known as "The Damascus Document," as Damascus was mentioned numerous times in the scroll.

Moving forward to 1947, a young Bedouin shepherd, Mohammad Al Deeb, was watching goats when he realized one was lost. The area, the mountainous Judean Wilderness, was filled with numerous caves, the perfect hiding place for a stray animal. On one steep hill was a cave that rose high—isolated and quite difficult to reach. The young shepherd began throwing stones inside the cave's opening, hoping to run the stray goat out of hiding. Suddenly, he heard a strange noise within the cave, as though the rock had hit something. After climbing the hill, he entered the cave and, to his amazement, discovered large clay jars with something rolled up inside that had the appearance and feel of some type of leather. The boy took the large rolls, then showed them and sold them to a Christian Arab merchant named Khalil Kando in Bethlehem. The purchaser hid the rolls and later showed them to an antiquities expert, who recognized them as ancient scrolls with writings. One was later confirmed to be the biblical book of Isaiah (chapters 16-66). Following this confirmation, searches were made in ten other caves during eight years. In the early 1950s, a strange discovery was made. A copy of the same document, found in Egypt in the late 1800s, was also hidden in one of the Qumran caves. This document appeared to also be a copy from a first-century document. The fact that these parchments were located in two places and held much of the same themes appeared to prove that the documents held important significance to the writers. Scholars believed the scroll was written in the time of Herod and expanded the Temple platform in Jerusalem a few years before Christ's birth. The message on the scroll was that Herod was an evil ruler, and the temple priesthood was corrupt.

WHAT IS THE DAMASCUS DOCUMENT?

Christian scholars point out that there is approximately 400 years of spiritual silence, or no prophetic voices, from the time of Malachi to the beginning of John the Baptist's ministry. Jewish history also notes that there was no significant prophetical voice during this time. The Damascus Document was believed to have been written by the men living in the Qumran community. While this section is not intended to expound on the identity or history of the men called Essenes who lived in the community, the main point of their dwelling in the isolation of the Judean desert is to highlight a life of separation and holiness, away from worldly influences. According to the information contained in numerous scrolls, the Essenes believed that the priesthood in Jerusalem was predicting and anticipating the arrival of a "teacher of righteousness."

It was about this same time when a prophet named John the Baptist appeared in public, baptizing believers in the Jordan River, which is located in the Jordan Rift Valley not far from Jericho in the Judean Wilderness. Luke's gospel reveals that John was in "in the deserts until the day of his showing" (Luke 1:80), and we know from biblical narratives that John's ministry activity was in the desert, not far from the Qumran area. This has caused some scholars to suggest that John actually lived among the Essenes in the vicinity of Qumran and may have been influenced by their life of separation and doctrine of holiness.

Why was the Damascus Document so important to those living in the Roman period of world history? Or more importantly, what does this writing have to do with those living at this present age? One reason I suggest it is important is because the document is apocalyptic in nature and often makes reference to the "last days."

When summing up some of the apocalyptic observations within this ancient document, it tells us that every biblical generation has had its righteous and its unrighteous remnant. Among the righteous were Noah, Abraham, and Moses. This theme continues when explaining how the larger population from the sons of Noah are considered in a fallen or a reprobate condition; yet, there is a faithful remnant that exists on the earth. One of the strong themes found among the Qumran community and penned in the scrolls is constant warfare between the Sons of Darkness and the Sons of Light. The Sons of Darkness are known as the sons of Belial, and there is a counter-religious leader, a righteous individual, called the "Teacher of Righteousness."

Some of the content of the Damascus Document related to the last days presents a picture of events that are unique in nature. The scroll predicts that a remnant of Jews will go to Damascus (in Syria) and find the tabernacle of David. There is also a story saying that the tabernacle and the Ark of the Covenant are hidden on Mount Nebo, the mountain where Moses last viewed the promised land prior to his death. This last point concerning the ark hidden in Mount Nebo is also mentioned in the book of 2 Maccabees, where it is written that Jeremiah hid it:

> "Having received an oracle, ordered that the tent and the ark should follow with him, and he went out to the mountain where Moses had gone up and hid the inheritance of God. Jeremiah came and found a cave-dwelling, and he brought there the tent and the ark and the altar of incense; then sealed up the entrance" (2 Maccabees 2:4-5).

The writer comments that the place will remain secret until God gathers his people together again and shows them mercy (2 Maccabees 2:7-8).

There are three key themes within the Damascus Document.

1. The final battle will be the Sons of Light against the Sons of Darkness.
2. Jerusalem's priesthood should replace animal sacrifices with prayers.
3. There is an expectation of divine intervention during the apocalyptic conflicts.

When we compare these themes with events and spiritual circumstances today, we can clearly observe the conflict brewing between those who walk in light and those who walk in darkness. The biblical parable of the wheat and tares is an example of the conflict between the children of the kingdom and the children of Satan (Matthew 13). Through the New Covenant in Christ, the blood offerings ceased as the final redemptive sacrifice was made by the lamb of God, Jesus Christ. Revelation 19 tells us that the Messiah will return with the armies of heaven to defeat all of God's enemies in an epic apocalyptic battle, the battle of Armageddon.

THE BIBLE AND DAMASCUS

Since 1948, about the only mention of Damascus was the wars previously fought with Israel, the two most noted: in 1967 and 1973. After losing the Golan Heights in 1967, the Syrian military forces in 1973 lost the Yom Kippur War, and since that time have basically ceased their major war conflicts with Israel. Yet, they have consistently challenged Israel politically and influenced nations to put pressure on Israel to return the Golan Heights back to Syria. At times, the buffer between Israel and Syria has been breached by terrorists with evil intent; they are almost always exposed and dealt with by the Israeli Defense Forces.

Damascus remained rather quiet, until rebels attempted to overthrow the Syrian president, Basher, with secret backing from the United States. A civil war ensued beginning in 2011, resulting in over 400,000 deaths and the displacement of hundreds of thousands of Syrians, now refugees, making their way to Europe and attempting to procure visas to the United States. Presently, the entire area of Syria seems to be one big war zone, and the war has gone to another level with the rise of a radical Islamic army called ISIS. The goal of ISIS is to reform a Caliphate, an Islamic empire in the heart of the Middle East with Damascus as its capital.

ISAIAH'S PREDICTION ABOUT DAMASCUS

With the turmoil in Syria, the involvement of Russia, and ISIS successfully seizing towns, beheading men, raping women, and killing Christians, the eyes of prophetic teachers and students have been centered on Syria and especially Damascus. The key Scriptures being observed with extreme interest are in Isaiah 17.

Isaiah released prophetic words, not only to his people in Jerusalem and Judea, but at times, his warnings extended to Gentile nations surrounding Israel too, including nations of influence in his day. For example, Isaiah 13 is a prophecy against Babylon, chapter 15 is a word against Moab, and chapter 18 is for a "land beyond Ethiopia." The prophet gives a warning of a civil war in Egypt and then remarks about the "burden of the sea" and speaks against Arabia. His entire seventeenth chapter, however, is a warning about the total destruction of Damascus. Isaiah states:

> "The burden of Damascus. Behold, Damascus is taken away from being a city, and it shall be a ruinous heap. The cities of Aroer are forsaken: they shall be for flocks, which shall lie down, and none shall make them afraid. The fortress also shall cease from Ephraim, and the kingdom from Damascus, and the remnant of Syria: they shall be as the glory of the children of Israel, saith the LORD of hosts" (Isaiah 17:1-3).

Damascus is one of the oldest continually inhabited cities in the Middle East, perhaps outside of Jericho, which is believed to be the oldest city on earth. Its name, Dimashq in Arabic, is derived from Dimashka, a word of pre-Semitic origin suggesting that the beginning of Damascus goes back to a time before recorded history. Damascus is mentioned in Genesis 14:15 as the city where Abraham's servant, Eliezer, is from. Damascus' greatest asset that prevented it from being destroyed and rebuilt numerous times is that the city was always an important oasis, a water source necessary for nomads and ancient travelers to water their flocks. In history, Damascus had its vineyards and orchards destroyed, but the city was spared of paying tribute.

In Isaiah 17, when Damascus is destroyed, Isaiah used three names that are not found in modern history and must be interpreted using the modern names of these regions. The first is Aroer, which is a place in south central Jordan today. The land of Ephraim is situated presently in the heart of what is called the West Bank in Israel. The remnant of Aram refers to the Syrian people. Thus, a part of Jordan will be forsaken, and the West Bank area is affected. The West Bank today is the center of the Palestinian conflict, and the majority living there are tied into Muslims in Lebanon and Syria. One of the reasons suggested that parts of southern Jordan are forsaken is because this part of Jordan borders Syria, and with the ISIS uprisings and civil wars in Syria, certain dangerous weapons may have been used, polluting the land or endangering inhabitants in the area. In Isaiah 17:4-9 a remnant will remain from this destruction.

In the Damascus prophecy, there may be several hints that indicate the circumstances of this destruction and perhaps the timing of the destruction.

> "Woe to the multitude of many people,
> which make a noise like the noise of
> the seas; and to the rushing of nations,
> that make a rushing like the rushing of
> mighty waters. The nations shall rush
> like the rushing of many waters: but God
> shall rebuke them, and they shall flee far
> off, and shall be chased as the chaff of
> the mountains before the wind, and like
> a rolling thing before the whirlwind. And
> behold at evening tide trouble; and before
> the morning he is not. This is the portion
> of them that spoil us, and the lot of them
> that rob us" (Isaiah 17:12-14).

The word "rushing" in Hebrew is *sha'own*, referring to a noise, but by implication referring to destruction. It indicates that at the time of the events, the nation will be angry. This would agree with Jesus who said, "Nation shall rise against nation and kingdom against kingdom" (Matthew 24:7) and John who wrote, "And the nations were angry" (Revelation 11:18). The trouble peaks at "evening tide," which would refer to later in the afternoon. However, notice that by morning, nothing exists.

Damascus should be one of those cities for which we should pray for the salvation of as many souls as possible and remain alert to the stunning predictions by Isaiah, which have not yet occurred but will in the future. It is interesting to research the many different scrolls, parchments, and documents that record end-time prophetic events and also to see how they correlate and agree with the inspired Word of God. These are just a few examples whose subject matter appears to align with the ancient scrolls of the biblical prophets.

11.

THE BATTLE OVER THE MOUNTAIN OF GOD—THE TEMPLE MOUNT CONTROVERSY

Why is Jerusalem such a focal point of conflict and controversy? It is a city shared by three monotheistic religions: Christianity, Judaism, and Islam. It is a popular tourist destination for all three religious groups, boasting of over 4 million visitors a year. So what makes this city—small in comparison to other cities—such a target for religious zealots and radical fanatics? We can safely say that Jerusalem is a city of contradictions and controversies. Three of these controversies that continue brewing are:

1. The controversy as to who is the rightful heir to the land of Israel
2. The controversy as to who owns the Temple Mount
3. The controversy as to who should have access to pray and worship on this mountain of God

The location of Jerusalem is central to the world, as

Ezekiel noted: "This is Jerusalem; I have set her in the midst (center) of the nations and the countries that are round about her" (Ezekiel 5:5). Ezekiel 38:12 describes Israel as dwelling "in the midst of the land" (KJV). The phrase can mean "the center of the world," or in Hebrew, "the navel of the world." In ages past, it appears that three continents—Europe, Africa, and Asia—were once joined as one land mass, as their coastlines to this day would fit together like a puzzle. Years ago, Dr. Andrew J. Woods, M.S., a physicist with Gulf Energy and Environmental Services in San Diego, proposed a six-part method to determine where the center of earth's landmass would be. He calculated that the probability that the earth's center would fall on the lands of the Bible would be one out of 450. His calculations revealed that the world's exact center was in Turkey, near Mount Ararat, where the ark rested after the flood. Thus, Noah's three sons had an equal opportunity to go out in three directions from the center of the known earth. Jerusalem is on the same latitude as Mount Ararat, 550 miles away.[32]

Rabbis have taught that Israel is the center of the world, Jerusalem the center of Israel, and the Temple Mount the center of Jerusalem. Just as in Eden, God set the tree of life in the midst (center) of the garden and met with man in that location each day (Genesis 2:9; 3:8-11). God set his holy mountain, called Mount Moriah, in the center of Jerusalem in the center of Israel to invite all men over twenty to join him during three main festivals each year.

The Temple Mount is called *Har Habayit* in Hebrew and *Harem esh-Sharif* in Arabic, meaning "the Noble Sanctuary." There is a tradition stating that when God created the heavens and the earth, he stood above the large stone (which is now exposed in the Islamic mosque, the Dome of the Rock) and spoke creation into existence. This lime-stone rock is ironically called "The Foundation Stone." There is a cave, part natural and part man-made, inside the Dome of the Rock, under a section of the founda-tion stone called the "Well of the Souls" or "Cave of the Spirits." The tradition of this cave dates back to medieval times, when it was said that from this cave a person can hear the spirits of the dead awaiting judgment. A cham-ber that exists under the marble floor has never been ex-cavated.

The white, rather flat, stone within the Islamic mosque, the Dome of the Rock, has been a source of controversy and speculation for centuries. Many devout Jews believe it was on this rock that Abraham built an altar and laid his son, Isaac, presenting him to God (see Genesis 22). This belief is enforced by the fact that God told Abraham to go to the land of Moriah on a mountain where he would show him and make his son a place on an altar (Genesis 22:1-2). The mountain of Moriah is also the mountain in which Solomon built the first Temple: "And Solomon be-gan to build the house of the LORD at Jerusalem in Mount Moriah, where the LORD appeared unto David his father, in the place David had prepared in the threshing floor of Ornan the Jebusite" (2 Chronicles 3:1).

The Chronicles narrative mentions David's involve-ment as "preparing the threshing floor of Ornan." This narrative is mentioned in two references. Toward the end of David's reign, the king committed a transgression when numbering the men in Israel and not collecting the half-shekel of redemption required by the law when num-bering men over twenty years of age (Exodus 30:12-14). A judgment angel with a large sword was prepared to de-stroy all men in Jerusalem. God opened the eyes of David, his elders, and Ornan to see the angry heavenly messenger bringing great fear to all. The angel spoke to the prophet Gad, instructing David to meet with Ornan, the owner of the threshing floor and instruments needed for harvesting wheat. David immediately offered 600 shekels of gold, purchasing the threshing floor and immediately constructing an altar to burn a sacrifice and amend his act of disobedience. The angel put away his sword, but a three-year famine resulted because of David's actions (see 1 Chronicles 21). It is interesting that Ornan was threshing wheat (1 Chronicles 21:20), which is the harvest assigned at the Festival of Pentecost. On that day, the fire of God fell from heaven on the altar and consumed the sacrifice and the altar. It would be over a thousand years later, on the Festival of Pentecost, that cloven tongues of fire from heaven would fall upon believers, baptizing them in God's Spirit (see Acts 2:1-4).

The Bible is clear that David *legally purchased the hill of Moriah* where his son Solomon built the first Jewish temple. Modern Islam rejects this fact and has gone as far as to deny that a Jewish presence was ever on the Temple Mount. However, most Muslims before 1948 believed there was an early Jewish presence on the Mount. For example, in 1871, a Holy Land explorer, Sir Richard Francis Burton, and his wife visited inside the Dome of the Rock and the Well of Souls. Muslims hosting him showed him the cave and a projecting stone point called a "tongue," in which they stated that the builder of the Dome, Omar, believed this was the rock identified as "Jacob's pillar" when he saw the vision of Bethel. If these Muslim guides believed this, they understood that a Jewish presence was linked to the place. Before 1948, numerous Islamic books and periodicals believed that the rock was once the Holy place in Solomon's temple. However, when Israel was re-established, history was concealed and rewritten to discourage any Jews from interest in the Temple Mount. This was because two mosques are built on the mountain. The main, and most notable, mosque, the Dome of the Rock, sits atop Mount Moriah and originally may have been a Byzantine Shrine before being remodeled in 691 B.C. A second mosque sits at the southern and lower part of Mount Moriah, the Al Aqsa Mosque, originally constructed in 705 A.D.

The Temple Mount has changed hands numerous times due to wars and conflicts between Muslims and Christians. The first exchange was in 1099 when the crusaders took Jerusalem and renamed Al Aqsa "Solomon's Temple" and the Dome of the Rock "Temple of God." Al Aqsa was used for a horse stable and became the headquarters for the Knights Templar, men who believed they were assigned to defend Jerusalem and the Holy places. Muslims under Saladin recaptured Jerusalem in 1187. Since that time the Temple Mount has basically remained in control of Islamic powers, and in modern times the nation of Jordan has served as the overseer of the Temple Mount. For many years, rumors that the Jews were planning to overtake the Mount, or pray on the mountain, caused violent riots to break out, as Palestinian youth clashed with Israeli police.

According to three specific New Testament references, there will be a temple on the Temple Mount at some point during the tribulation. The first reference is made by Christ when he declared, "When ye therefore shall see the abomination of desolation, spoken of by Daniel the prophet, stand in the holy place (whoso reads, let him understand); then let them which be in Judea flee into the mountains" (Matthew 24:15-16). At the time of Matthew's writing he was uncertain as to just what this abomination was. However, years later, John revealed that a false prophet would make an image of the beast, causing it to speak and live, demanding people to worship the image. This would signal Jews fleeing into the wilderness (Revelation 12:1-18; 13:11-19). This image is an idol, and all idolatry is an "abomination" before God. The second reference to a temple is when Paul revealed the rise of the Antichrist and said, "He as God will sit in the temple of God showing himself that he is God" (2 Thessalonians 2:4). This "temple" is not a metaphor for the human body or the church, as some interpret it. This is a visible temple in Jerusalem that will be constructed by the two witnesses of the first half of the tribulation (Revelation 11:1-2). At mid-point in the tribulation, the Antichrist will enter Jerusalem, taking over half the city (see Zechariah 14:1-2), and part of his activity will be to stop any Jewish presence on the Temple Mount. As Daniel noted, "In the midst of the week (or middle of seven-year tribulation), he (the Antichrist) will cause the sacrifice to cease" (Daniel 9:27). The third temple reference is in Revelation, when John is told to "measure the Temple of God and they that worship therein," but not to measure the outer court as it is "given to the Gentiles," who will trample the city for a final forty-two months (see Revelation 11).

Some have suggested that a Jewish temple could be built anywhere in Israel and not just in Jerusalem on the Temple Mount. This is not correct. A Jewish synagogue could be built anywhere in the land, but a synagogue is not the Temple. A synagogue is a gathering or assembly place for the community to pray and study. The Temple is the center for celebrating the major festivals—bringing tithes and offerings and worshipping with instruments and music.

The rebuilding of this Temple that, according to Israeli professors such as Asher Kauffman, will require forty-two months to construct because special prayers and cleansing rituals are required, will become the trigger for the Antichrist and his forces to rise up and retake half of Jerusalem (east Jerusalem), which was once in the hands of Jordan and is predominantly Muslim. Once the Antichrist invades Jerusalem, he would be hailed as a hero in the Muslim world for "liberating" the mountain from any Jewish presence.

WHO OWNS THE LAND OF ISRAEL?

If you examine any map of the Middle East in any Arab or Islamic nation, no map says "Israel." The land Israel now possesses is identified on the maps as "Palestine." The conflict concerning the name of this land and who is the true owner is far more complex than one chapter in a book can explain. To simplify the controversy, basically the internal conflicts and external pressure placed on Israel stems from three points of view, predominantly expressed from those who identify themselves as "Palestinians."

1. In 1947, the United Nations voted to partition (carve out) a portion of land in Palestine for a new Jewish state. For non-Jews living in Palestine, this was viewed as a hostile takeover. Jews were being supported by the Christian West, occupying land owned by Arabs whose previous generations lived in Palestine prior to 1948. Thus, to those identi-

fying themselves as "Palestinian people," the Jews live in an "illegal" nation by building cities and settlements on property that is not theirs.

2. The Six Day War was June 5-10, 1967, when Israel defeated the armies of three surrounding nations: Egypt, Jordan, and Syria. Egyptian forces were amassing near Israel's border in the Sinai Peninsula, threatening to attack. Israel pre-empted an air strike, decimating the Egyptian air force and later defeating Egyptian and Syrian tank brigades in the south and the north. Jordan was pulled into the war by threats made to the Jordanian leadership by President Nasser in Egypt. This stretched the conflict into Jerusalem, a city divided between Jordan and Israel. After the war victory, Israel annexed east Jerusalem, ancient Judea, Samaria (called the West Bank), the Gaza Strip, and the Golan Heights. They later gave the Sinai Peninsula, a large chunk of land between Israel and Egypt, back to Egypt in a peace treaty that was signed at the White House on March 26, 1979, and initiated by U.S. President Carter, Israeli Prime Minister Menachem Begin, and President Anwar Sadat of Egypt. Israel, however, held on to the West Bank and Golan Heights, mainly for security purposes. Many in the Muslim world use these annexations as proof that the Jews are occupiers in the Holy Land and should be forced to leave and settle in Europe or America.

3. Jerusalem is the main root of all conflict. Jerusalem is shared by three religions: Christianity, Judaism, and Islam. Christians have no problem sharing the city with other religions, and by-in-

large, Jews co-exist with other Muslims in the city. However, there is a percentage of Muslims who believe that their assignment is to forcibly expel both Jews and Christians out of Jerusalem since these two religions surround the third holiest site in Islam, the mountain where the two mosques sit. Both religions also disagree with certain concepts and teachings promoted in the Islamic religion.

Among the biblically knowledgeable Jews, there is no question as to who owns the land of Israel. The Bible indicates that the landmass from the river of Egypt to the Euphrates was promised to the seed of Abraham, through Isaac, which are the Hebrew people (Genesis 15:8). This land grant promise was sealed by God through a blood covenant with Abraham and his descendants, being passed on through Isaac, Jacob, and his twelve sons, all of whom were marked by circumcision, the sign of the covenant (Genesis 17:11), and all of whom assisted in forming the nation of Israel.

Among Christian groups, there is a division as to who owns the land. Many Evangelical-Pentecostal-Charismatic ministers and their congregations often interpret the Scriptures in a more literal sense, and most acknowledge the Jewish right not only to a homeland, but also to live and thrive in the very land today called Israel. However, Israel's "thorn in their flesh," so to speak, is the many Muslims in and outside of Israel who believed that the Jews have been occupying Islamic land since their beginning as a modern nation in 1948.

The idea of Jews being occupiers in the land is seldom taught publicly in America, perhaps due to the large number of Jews living in America (5.3 million) and support

that Israel has received from America's Christian community. This support is not a blind-cart blank support base,
but it is rooted in the knowledge of the Bible, the promises
given to Abraham, the biblical covenants, and the fulfillment of end-time prophecies occurring in Israel and Jerusalem. Among the majority of Muslims, especially in the
Middle East, there is a common theme that Israel was a
nation formed by the West and has no legal right in the
eyes of Allah (God) to exist. Thus, it becomes the duty of
every Muslim to support any jihad (holy war) against the
Jews—not only in Israel, but anywhere in the world.

THE QURAN VERSES—ISRAEL'S LAND

What is strange is that there are certain verses in the Quran that teach that the Jews have the right to the land and
that God would bring them back. A professor of religious
studies at San Diego State University was interviewed for
FrontPage Magazine in 2004. The professor quoted from the
Quran, Chapter 5:20-21, in which Moses said, "O my
people! Remember the bounty of God upon you when
he bestowed prophets upon you, and made you kings and
gave you that which had not been given to anyone before
you amongst the nations. O my people! Enter the Holy
Land which God has written for you, and do not turn tail,
otherwise you will be losers." The professor noted that this
passage says that the Holy Land was given to the Jews.
The professor, Abdul Hadi Palazzi, has served as a lec-
turer in the Department of History at the University of
Velletri in Rome, Italy.

Professor Abdul Hadi Palazzi quoted passages from the
Quran from "Night Journey" chapters 17:100-104, where
Moses is confronting Pharaoh. The professor comments,

"God wanted to give Abraham a double blessing through Ishmael and through Isaac and ordered that Ishmael's descendants should live in the desert of Arabia and Isaac's in Canaan." He continues, "The Quran recognized the land of Israel as the heritage of the Jews, and it explains that, before the Last Judgment, Jews will return to dwell there. This prophecy has already been fulfilled."[33]

The professor's theory is further expressed when stating that the earth belongs to the Lord, and "he is free to entrust sovereignty over land to whomsoever he likes for whatever time period that he chooses." The professor continues to quote from the Quran, revealing a verse that is totally ignored by Islamic radicals, seeing the destruction of Israel and the death of Jews. The verse reads:

> "And (remember) when Moses said to his people: 'O my people, call in remembrance the favor of God unto you, when he produced prophets among you, made you kings, and gave you what He had not given to any other among the peoples. O my people, enter the Holy Land which God has assigned unto you, and turn not back ignominiously, for then will ye be overthrown, to your own ruin" (Quran 5:20-21).

Perhaps the most interesting Quranic passage used to show that Jews will have the land of Israel before the last judgment is found in Quran 17:104: "And thereafter We (Allah) said to the children of Israel; 'Dwell securely in the promised land. And when the last warning will come to pass, we will gather you in a mingled crowd." The professor noted a statement made by King Faisal, a former king of Iraq, who commented, "The Arabs and particularly the educated ones among them, must look to the Zionist movement with the deepest sympathy." In 1919 Faisal met with Dr. Chaim Weizmann, president of the Zionist Organization, and signed an agreement with this Jewish group, in which the respected Arab leader accepted the Balfour Declaration, a document that promised that the British would support a homeland for the Jews in Palestine. Thus, before 1948, many Jews and Arabs were friends, and Jews lived in Persia (Iran), Iraq, Lebanon, and northern Africa. After Israel was reestablished, many Muslims believed their holy places in Jerusalem were in danger, and some began a war against the Jews attempting to prevent not only their immigration back to Israel, but also their permanent settling in the land.

These statements clearly indicate that there is written in Islam's main holy book, the Quran, statements indicating that the Jews have the rights to the Holy Land (Israel), and Jews will be dwelling in their promised land (Israel) in the last days.[34]

Since Muslims accept the Quran as inspired, why do they seem to ignore these predictions that favor Jews owning the land? The reason: the majority of Muslims do not read the Quran, as it is written in the Arabic language, and many Muslims refuse to read other translations outside of the original Arabic version. Most of the Quranic interpretations are derived from imams (preachers) in their mosques. Thus, if the imam is a peaceful person, the people often reflect the same. If the imam is radical, outspoken, and a pro-jihadi against the West and Israel, the attendees will take on a similar spirit. In the Quran are peace verses and dangerous war verses, and depending upon the type of Islamic interpretation and Islam the people practice, the Quran can be used by Muslims to either promote peace or to promote jihad against Christians and Jews. I personally believe that if there were not two Islamic mosques on the Temple Mount in Jerusalem, and the legend of a "night journey" that modern Muslims believe occurred in Jerusalem did not exist, then most of the world's Muslims would have little interest in Jerusalem or the Temple area.

THE CONTROVERSY OF THE TEMPLE MOUNT

In February 638 A.D., the Islamic caliph Omar entered Jerusalem riding on a white camel. As Omar rode to the Temple Mount, he was with the patriarch Sophronius, the chief magistrate. It is said that the patriarch began weeping and quoted the prophecy of Daniel: "Behold the abomination of desolation spoken of by the prophet" (Daniel 11:31). Omar would later clear the area of trash and debris, building a wooden mosque over what was believed to be the foundation of a Christian church. This would eventually become the Dome of the Rock.

More fanatical Muslims teach that the Jews never had control of the Mount and that the two Jewish temples never existed. While the name Jerusalem is never mentioned in the Quran, Muslims speak of a night journey that Mohammad took from Mecca to "the furthest mosque" on his horse, Barak. The Quran reads, "I declare the glory of him who transported his servant by night from the Masjid al Haram (the mosque at Mecca) to the Masjid al Aksa (the further mosque) at Jerusalem" (Quran 17:1). Muslims believe Mohammad went to Jerusalem, where he met Moses, Jesus, and other prophets, then returned to his

Muslim followers. Muslims teach that Mohammad was on his winged steed called Al Barak, meaning "the lightning," escorted by the angel Gabriel. Devout Muslims have even pointed out indentions on a rock, protected by a small black box inside the Dome of the Rock. They consider these the footprints Mohammad's horse left when ascending from the mosque.

Omar in 635 caused the domed mosque to be built on what was believed to be the ancient site of the first Temple. Omar discovered a large rock underneath a dung hill and prayed there, dedicating the rock for a mosque. The famous golden Dome of the Rock was eventually built in 691 A.D. by Caliph Abed el-Malik. The plans were copied from a fourth century Christian shrine on the Mount of Olives. It is believed the site was built as a counter attraction to the two main Islamic mosques in Arabia: Mecca and Medina.

Some Islamic scholars, such as Egyptian commentator Ahmed Mahmad Oufa, wrote that the verse mentioned in the Quran about the night journey has nothing to do with Jerusalem. He instead referred to a mosque that was located near the city of Medina in Mohammad's time since Islam was so young and had not yet spread to Jerusalem, which was basically at time in ruins.

Not only is there clear biblical evidence that the Jews have the historical ownership of the mountain, we also have a record in the Bible where David purchased the mountain from Ornan the Jebusite, paying him in both gold and silver (see 2 Samuel 24 and 1 Chronicles 21). After David's death, Solomon built the first Jewish Temple on the sacred mountain of Moriah, and the Bible records a complete record of Solomon's building program—the cost and a vivid description (1 Kings 6-7). Over 900 years later, Jesus is ministering at the Jerusalem's "second" Temple. This Temple is mentioned throughout the New Testament, and a detailed description is given by the eyewitness historian Flavius Josephus. This noted Jewish historian also gives a detailed eyewitness account of the destruction of the Temple by the Roman Tenth Legion in his lengthy document called *Wars of the Jews*.

After the 1967 war, a professor from the Hebrew University, Asher Kaufman, walked on the Temple Mount, photographing visible evidence of steps, Roman stones, and remnants of Herod's Temple. After realizing his photographs could be used as evidence of an ancient Jewish presence, the Islamic authorities literally dug up and removed every piece of visible evidence of any possible Jewish temple from the mountain. Because Islamic leaders refuse to excavate on the Temple Mount, the tons of debris that would reveal the actual foundation stones of the ancient temples are concealed underground. However, several years ago, tons of dirt was taken from the mount and dumped outside the walls. Today there is an organization sifting through the dirt, occasionally discovering interesting artifacts that prove that the Jews lived in Jerusalem. These artifacts include coins and images of the menorah. Archeologists have also found evidence that would date back to the time of Solomon (first Temple period) and the Roman time (second Temple period).

ARCHEOLOGY AND THE JEWISH PRESENCE

The temple vessels used by the priests were to be made of stone, not clay, partially for ritual purposes. According to Jewish writings such as the Talmud and Mishna, it was believed that water from a stone vessel was ritualistically pure. I collect authentic ancient relics from Israel, some dating back as far as 3,500 years. I obtained a small cup with a spout that was discovered in Jerusalem. It was carved out of limestone, and Jewish antiquities dealers say that it was possibly a stone cup used for measuring water, oil, or some liquid at the Temple. There have been stones with writings, parchments, ancient seals, pottery, and coins found in excavations, indicating that the Jews certainly did have possession of Jerusalem long before the Gentile powers seized control. One of the very visible pieces of evidence of a Jewish presence is the numerous Mik'vot, ritual pools that were carved directly into the limestone rock. These pools were used in the second Temple period for attendees to submerge themselves in before entering the sacred Temple at the southern steps.

Thus, the controversy continues. Was there a Jewish Temple, or is it all a lie? If there was, do devout Jews want their Temple Mount back? What would the Muslims do with the Al Asqua Mosque and the Dome of the Rock if there were a Jewish presence? It is clear that many Muslims are becoming fearful that the Jews will one day seize the Temple Mount to build a new Temple, helping to fulfill certain Jewish traditions as a sign to bring the Messiah.

THE CONTROVERSY OF THE TEMPLE

Through the centuries, since the destruction of the Jewish Temple, the Temple Mount has been a hot spot of controversy. This hill of the Lord since 70 A.D. has changed ownership between the Romans to the Byzantines, the Byzantines to the Muslims, the Muslims to crusaders, and back and forth. From 1517 to 1917 Palestine was under Islamic Turkish rule, until the British liberated Palestine, placing it under the British Mandate.

When Israel became a nation in 1948, the Temple Mount remained in the possession of the Muslims. Even after the 1967 war, when Israeli paratroopers and troops drove onto the Temple Mount planting an Israeli flag on top, just above the Western Wall, the flag was immediately removed and later Israeli Defense Minister Moshe Dayan removed all Israeli paratroopers from the Mount, giving total control back to the Muslim keepers. Israel feared an all-out major war with surrounding Muslim nations if they attempted to maintain control of Muslim-controlled property. Despite this fact, until recently, Jews were not permitted to go on top of the Mount for fear of retaliation from Muslims and restrictions by the head rabbis. Even recently, Christian groups were removed for discussing a Jewish presence that was once on the Mount, and Bible reading is forbidden.

In 1985, during my first trip to Israel, I inquired about Jewish interest in a new temple. The answers were vague and often mechanical, such as "We don't need one today" or "The spirit of the nation is its temple." Today, however, over 58 percent of Jews living in Israel would like to again see a temple in Jerusalem. This change in attitude has brought concern to many Muslims leaders.

This concern was demonstrated years ago when Yasser Arafat traveled to Indonesia, the world's largest Islamic nation, and held up a photograph on live television. The picture was an aerial view of Jerusalem with the dome removed and a computer-generated image of the Jewish Temple in its place. Using this as "evidence," Arafat warned that the Jews had a plan to destroy the Dome of the Rock and in its place construct their own temple. This photograph was actually a picture sold to tourists that shows what Jerusalem looked like in the time of Christ with Herod's Temple sitting on the mount. It was not intended to promote a new temple.

A CALL FROM A COLONEL

I personally am a witness to how swift a controversy can brew, especially through visual media. Years ago, I taped two programs, one in front of an abandoned tank in the Golan Heights and the second in front of the Eastern Gate in a Muslim cemetery. During the Golan message, I compared a new Israeli tank, the Merkaba (a Hebrew word found in the Bible meaning "chariot") with possible prophetic Scriptures in Nahum. I shared some of the details about this tank, as I had just been on an Israeli base where I was shown the tank and intrigued how the old word *chariot* was now a new weapon that jumped over hills and shot fiery missiles. In the second taping I shared the "secrets under the Temple Mount," including the rumor that the Ark of the Covenant was concealed in a small cavern. This story was told to me by a head rabbi who allegedly saw the ark in a very deteriorated condition and kept it concealed in this chamber to prevent an Islamic uprising in Jerusalem.

When both programs aired, I received a call from a retired American colonel, who was asked by the Israeli representative from the United Nations and a member of the Clinton State Department to call and rebuke me for sharing "sensitive information" on global television, including insight into Israeli military equipment. He said Muslims had downloaded the programs and were distributing them in various nations, and it was creating a problem. I was asked never to air those two programs again, which we never did. I would never dream that discussing the Temple Mount and a piece of Israeli military weaponry (now publicly seen and discussed) would generate such a dispute.

It is clear that devout and more radicalized Muslims would prefer for any Jew not to be living in Israel, and Israel is considered Palestinian land that Jews are "occupying." Muslims worldwide, however, would agree that the Temple Mount belongs only to them as Jerusalem is considered Islam's third holiest site, just behind Mecca and Medina in Saudi Arabia.

Despite this global opposition, the New Testament indicates that a Jewish temple will again exist in Jerusalem in the same location as the previous ones. How is this possible, considering that the laws of Islam would never allow a Jewish temple to be built on the same location?

THEORIES RELATED TO THE
DOME'S DESTRUCTION

There are three main theories presented by prophetic teachers who acknowledge that a future temple in Jerusalem will be built during the tribulation. These theories also address what will happen to the Dome of the Rock.

1. THE DOME WILL BE DESTROYED
BY AN EARTHQUAKE

The first theory insists that an earthquake in Jerusalem will destroy both mosques. Earthquakes have occurred for 1,600 years in the region and damaged the Dome of the Rock on several occasions, including in 808 and 1016, when the Dome collapsed. It was rebuilt, though, in 1021.

Other earthquakes have done minor damage. Revelation 11 predicts an earthquake in Jerusalem so devastating that one-tenth of the city will be destroyed and 7,000 men will be killed (Revelation 11:13). However, this occurs after a temple has been constructed and not before, as a temple is rebuilt in the first forty-two months of the tribulation, and this earthquake happens at the mid-tribulation point. If an earthquake leveled the mosque, the Israelis would not come in to scrape up the debris. The Muslims would repair it since by Islamic law once a mosque has been built it becomes the property of Islam forever. Earthquakes will happen, but this is not the key to constructing another Jewish temple in the future.

2. THE DOME WILL BE MOVED

This theory is so farfetched that it requires immediate rejection, yet some teachers continue suggesting it. Several Jewish businessmen have suggested that the Dome could be dismantled and moved to Arabia or another Islamic nation. In this way the mount is cleared for a Jewish temple in the tribulation. There is no historic record of any major Islamic mosque being dismantled and moved to another nation. In this case, Jerusalem is the third holiest site, and this would also require the dismantling of the Al Aqsa mosque, a rectangular building that is 144,000 square meters (1,550,000 square feet) and can hold up to 5,000 worshipers. It is located on the southern end of the mount; the original structure began as a small prayer building in 705. This mosque was severely damaged by an earthquake in 1033 but was rebuilt two years later.

In 1969 an Australian tourist, Denis Rohan, started a fire in the Al Aqsa mosque on the Temple Mount, hoping to burn it down to hasten the return of Christ and allowing the Jews to rebuild their temple. A second attack was in the 1980s when a Jewish underground group plotted to explode the Al Aqsa and the Dome to awaken the spirit of the Jewish people to rebuild the Third Temple in Jerusalem on the sacred mountain.

In the 1930s and again in the early 1990s there were repairs made on the building, and some of the older wood was removed and replaced with new wood. Radiocarbon dating revealed they were cedars of Lebanon, and the carbon dating placed the wood as far back as the ninth century B.C. I recall being on the Temple Mount when old pieces of wood were lying on the ground from inside the mosque, and I was told by our tour guide (Gideon) that the wood was believed by his Jewish sources to have been wood previously used in the Temple of Solomon that had survived the destruction. It had then been reused in Herod's Temple and later cleaned and reused in the building of the early mosque in the eighth century. I was also told that a Jewish businessman was purchasing the old wood from those repairing the mosque and was storing it in a safe place in Israel. Back to the theory being discussed, no Muslim would ever permit any mosque in Jerusalem to be dismantled or moved under any condition, unless Muslims were repairing or remodeling the structure.

3. THE DOME WILL CO-EXIST ALONG WITH THE TEMPLE

This theory is the only one that can be proven in prophetic Scripture. We find the clue in Revelation chapter 11. In John's vision, he is instructed to measure the Temple of God and the court where the people are worshipping, but to omit measuring the outer court: "Then I was given a reed like a measuring rod. And the angel stood, saying, 'Rise and measure the temple of God, the altar, and those who worship there. But leave out the court which is outside the temple, and do not measure it, for it has been given to the Gentiles. And they will tread the holy city underfoot for forty-two months" (Revelation 11:1-2 (NJKV)).

This was written twenty-five years after Jerusalem's temple was destroyed. Thus, it does not refer, as some suggest, to the Temple of John's day. Neither does it refer to the heavenly temple where God dwells, as this temple will never be "trodden down of Gentiles." This is a clear allusion to the Jewish temple rebuilt during the great tribulation, which is overseen by the two witnesses God will send, referred to in Revelation 11. Note in the prophecy that the temple and altar are measured, but the outer court is omitted and "given to the Gentiles," who will trample the city for forty-two months, referring to the final three and a half years of the tribulation.

Having been to Jerusalem thirty-five times and studied this text for years, I know that the Temple Mount will eventually be divided into two sections—one section given to the Gentiles (where the two mosques are), and the northern section, a large empty place today, will be handed over to a Jewish remnant. This could be accomplished in a treaty signed after the notable war of Gog of Magog, in which Israel decimates entire Islamic armies, leaving only one-sixth remaining (Ezekiel 39:1-2). A second point is that when the two witnesses (Enoch and Elijah) set their headquarters in Jerusalem for forty-two months, the first half of the tribulation, their ministry is confirmed with stunning and frightening signs and wonders, including withholding rain for forty-two months and calling fire from heaven on distractors. These signs would bring fear in the hearts of especially Muslims, thus allowing them to proceed with preparations, plans, and procedures to construct a temple (Revelation 11:1-6). Of course, the Antichrist will storm into Jerusalem with his Islamic hordes, killing the witnesses about the time that the temple dedication would occur, "causing the sacrifice to cease" (Daniel 9:27). Israeli researchers believe it would require exactly forty-two months, not to construct a temple but to have it prepared according to ancient rituals, prayers, and festivals, for actual worship.

In the early 1990s Pastor Mike Coleman related to me a special meeting he had with Professor Kauffman of Hebrew University. Years earlier they discussed the rebuilding of a temple on the Temple Mount in Jerusalem. The professor related that the materials for the building and the actual construction process would not take that long; however, because certain prayer and Jewish rituals must be performed on feast days, new moons, and Sabbaths, it would take about forty-two months from initiating the process to the completion. He also indicated that a temple would be dedicated on Passover. Today, several small groups and noted organizations have been researching the idea of a future temple, and some have made their own preparations for such.

THE ORGANIZING OF THE TEMPLE INSTITUTE

One such organization's headquarters in Jerusalem is the Temple Institute. Founded by Rabbi Yisrael Ariel in 1987, the rabbi served in the paratrooper brigade, which liberated the Temple Mount during the 1967 war. The organization is dedicated to researching, building, and restoring the sacred vessels used in the Temple. The institute houses numerous vessels that are, according to some, more than models or simple museum replicas. These gold, silver, and brass articles can actually be used in the next temple. The institute has studied and researched each item using the Torah, Jewish commentaries, ancient carvings, and historical documents.

More recently, the institute completed the garments of the high priest, the table of shewbread, the golden altar, and the menorah. The giant six-foot replica of the menorah is located in the Jewish quarter, protected behind glass. The only sacred item the institute has not worked on is the famed Ark of the Covenant. This may be because of the belief that the ark is still hidden under the Temple Mount.

THE TEMPLE MOUNT FAITHFUL

Another smaller, rather fringe group headed by Gershon Solomon is called the "Temple Mount Faithful." According to their website, templemountfaithful.org, their primary goal is the "building of the third temple on the Temple Mount in Jerusalem in our lifetime in accordance with the Word of G-d and all the Hebrew prophets and the liberation of the Temple Mount from Arab (Islamic) occupation so that it may be consecrated to the Name of G-d."

On several occasions, a small group of the faithful made news in Israel by attempting to move a large limestone rock onto the Temple Mount, calling it the "cornerstone of the next temple." The movement was stopped, and the stone was never permitted to enter the temple compound. This group is committed to the rebuilding of the Third Temple.

THE RE-ORGANIZATION OF THE SANHEDRIN

In the time of the second Temple, the Sanhedrin, the "Jewish Supreme Court," consisting of seventy-one older sages, was the most important judicial body in Christ's time. There was a Sanhedrin consisting of twenty-three members in every city of Israel in early times. There was also the Great Sanhedrin consisting of seventy-one older sages, the seventy-first member being the high priest himself. Their last decision was made in 358 A.D. when the Hebrew calendar was adopted. Severe persecution by the Romans drove the Sanhedrin out of existence. After being gone for 1,500 years, the Sanhedrin was reformed in Tiberius, Israel, in October 2004, with dozens of rabbis. Rabbi Israel Ariel of the Temple Institute is one of the participating rabbis.

The concept of the Sanhedrin dates back to the time of Moses, when God instructed the prophet to assemble seventy men of the elders of Israel. We read in the Torah where Moses and the seventy elders went to the top of the mountain to meet with God (Exodus 24). It is significant that this group has reorganized, although there are numerous rabbis who believe the group is invalid until the Messiah returns.

RETURN OF THE CRIMSON WORM

It seems strange that to rebuild a temple certain sacred compounds and items must be found that were part of the previous two temples. One such component required for the scarlet threads used by the high priest on the Day of Atonement and necessary for the burning of a red heifer (ritual purification) as well as needed for the dye to color the sixteen-meter-long belt for the priestly garments is the *tola'at shani,* or crimson worm. The "worm" is not actually a worm at all but a tiny insect that produces eggs on the bark of a tree that must be harvested at a certain time to secure the red color pigment contained in the eggs, used for the dye needed. After the eggs dry, they can be boiled in water, and the red dye is released. The Temple Institute in Jerusalem set out on a mission to discover the source of the red dye needed for the temple services. Research was made in Turkey and South America where the red dye was used for a food coloring. But to the amazement of Professor Zohar Amar, researcher, he discovered that the insect creates the eggs needed on oak trees in Samaria, in Israel. He has since demonstrated to students how this dye is created, and today the Temple Institute in Jerusalem is producing the 120 garments needed for future temple service.[35]

These simple preparations are early indicators of an interest in the rebuilding of the Jewish Temple. The New Testament predictions in Matthew 24:15, 2 Thessalonians 2:4, and Revelation 11:1-2 are not allegories and metaphors, as believed by some who do not accept the fact of a literal temple being rebuilt. While how the scenario will unfold remains a mystery, the Scriptures must be fulfilled—and will be in the future. The fact remains, there is a temple in Jerusalem during the tribulation! (Revelation 11:1-6)

12.

WHAT DOES ALL
OF THIS MEAN?

I believe that certain biblical, prophetic revelations concerning the end of days at times can only be understood and interpreted as the end of days approaches. For example, in the book of Revelation there are several remarkable predictions listed that in John's day would have been impossible, not only to occur, but also to understand. The visionary speaks of an army of two hundred thousand, thousand, or a 200-million-man army marching across the Euphrates, which numerically could not, and did not, exist in his day (Revelation 9:14-16). Even the Roman army in John's day would have boasted of no more than several hundred thousand throughout the empire. Only in our time could nations such as China or India produce an army of 200 million troops. The drying of the Euphrates will be due to a long drought; however, Turkey has several dams that can now control the water flow and water level of the Euphrates, making it is possible to actually dry up the entire flow into Syria and Iraq.

Consider the mark of the beast in which all people will be required to have a mark, name, or number on their right hand or forehead to control buying and selling (Revelation 13:17-18). How could this be possible in John's day? However, with computers, biometric scanners, invisible tattoos, pen numbers, and new technology, this is not only possible, but some tech companies are working on *cashless systems* similar to what we read about in John's stunning vision. Globalists are promoting a cashless society in which cards would be replaced with either a chip under the skin or an invisible tattoo on the skin, with personal information that can be scanned directly into stores or your bank. Much can actually be done using a phone. Centuries ago, older scholars had no idea how universal selling and buying would occur using numbers; however, today it is occurring in many forms.

A third verse is when John penned that at the return of Christ, "every eye shall see him" (Revelation 1:7). Due to the fact that the Roman Empire spread into the Middle East and Europe and that communication had to be hand delivered via scroll, how would this be possible? Christ did not return in John's time, nor in any previous age, but he will in the future. Our generation now has the visual technology, with satellite, Facebook, and other forms of visual communication—not just through television but now on phones—that literally, at his visible return to earth, touching down in Jerusalem on the Mount of Olives (Zechariah 14:4; Revelation 19:11-14), "every eye could see him."

This brings me to the use of the Hebraic alphabet, numbers, and the methods known by Jewish rabbis. I believe this is another level and layer of prophetic knowledge that is just being understood in the West, yet was known in John's day (Revelation 13:17-18) and used occasionally throughout Jewish history for at least 2,500 years: "But you, Daniel, shut up the words, and seal the book until the time of the end; many shall run to and fro, and knowledge shall increase" (Daniel 12:4 (NKJV)).

The understanding of Daniel's prophecies was to be "shut up" (sealed, KJV) unto the time of the end. This indicates that an increase in prophetic understanding will be released in the end of days, and prophetic mysteries that were once concealed will be revealed. Without doubt, we are the "revelation generation," blessed to understand and interpret both simple and detailed prophecies, unlock the symbolism, and peel back various layers of understanding to behold a complete picture. As said in the beginning, we are in the age of the Candelabra, as the prophecies related to Christ's return have been set in motion since 1948.

ENDNOTES

1. Josephus: *Antiquities of the Jews; War of the Jews;* Book VI; chapter 5
2. Josephus: *Antiquities of the Jews; War of the Jews;* Book VI; chapter 5, section III
3. www.globalresearch.ca/how-many...lost-their-home-us.../5335430
4. Jasher, chapters 4 and 5
5. Rabbi Ben Samuel, *Sefer Gematriot*
6. www.agrexco.com/Israels_Agricultural_Technology
7. www.biblebelievers.org.au?expelled.thm
8. en.wikipedia.org/wiki/WesternWall
9. dnr.mo.gov/geology/geosrv/geores/techbullitin1.htm
10. Josephus: *Antiquities of the Jews, War of the Jews, Seige of Jerusalem;* Book V, VI, and VII
11. Adam Clark, *New Testament Commentary on Matthew 6:24*
12. www.diffen.com/difference/Democracy_vs_Re-

public

13. www.vroma.org/-bncmanus/socialclass.html

14. www.Jasoncolavito/.../the-prophecy-of-adam-and-the-pillar-or-table

15. *cf. Herodotus, Hist. i.128,iii.132.2,151.1)*

16. en.wikipedia.org/.../Demographic_history_of_Jerusalem

17. www.hebrewtoday.com/content/Hebrew-alpha-bet-letter-zayin

18. www.breakingisraelnews.com/78667/trump-prophesied-leader

19. www.nas.gov.uk/about/090401, the National Archives of Scotland

20. Rev. B. Murphy, *Precursory Proofs that the Israelites came from Egypt and Ireland,* 1816

21. Rev. J. W. Brooks, *Jewish Chronicles,* 1828

22. www.ensignmessage.com/nobleorigins.htlm

23. Henry Guinness, *The Approaching End of the Age,* Preface to Second Edition, pp. xx-xxii

24. Henry Guinness, *Approaching End of the Age,* p. 94, par. 2 and 3

25. Henry Guinness, *Approaching the End of the Age,* pp. 298-299

26. William B. Godbey, A.M., *Godbey's Commentary,* Vol. I Revelation

27. William B. Godbey, A.M., *Godbey's Commentary,* Vol. 1 Revelation, pp. 66-67

28. bible.org/seriespage/1-basicconsiderations-inter-pretingprophecy

29. Noah was 500 when Shem, Ham, and Japeth were born (Genesis 5:30).

30. Vendall Jones, *The Researcher Magazine,* November 1996

31. Robert Wiseman and Michael Wise, *The Dead Sea Scrolls Uncovered*, Introduction, 1972, p. 10
32. Henry M. Morris, Ph.D, "The Center of the Earth," www.icr/articles/50/article
33. www.templemount.org/guranland.html
34. Shaykh Prof. Abdul Hadi Palazzi, "What the Quran Really Says," www.templemount.org/quranland.html
35. www.templeinstitute.org/tola-at_shani.htm